# A Treatise on Irresistible Grace, and Other Sermons

By John Preston

with chapters by C. Matthew McMahon

# Copyright Information

*A Treatise on Irresistible Grace, and Other Sermons*, by John Preston, with chapters by C. Matthew McMahon
Edited by Therese B. McMahon

Copyright © 2024 by Puritan Publications and A Puritan's Mind

Some language and grammar has been updated from the original manuscript. Any change in wording or punctuation has not changed the intent or meaning of the original author(s), and has been made to aid the modern reader.

Published by Puritan Publications
A Ministry of A Puritan's Mind
Crossville, TN
www.puritanpublications.com
www.apuritansmind.com

All rights reserved. No part of this publication may be reproduced, stored in a retrieval system or transmitted in any form by any means, electronic, mechanical, photocopy, recording or otherwise, without the prior permission of the publisher, except as provided by USA copyright law.

This Printed Edition, 2024
Manufactured in the United States of America

eISBN: 978-1-62663-482-4
ISBN: 978-1-62663-483-1

# Table of Contents

Meet John Preston ................................................................. 4

Introduction .......................................................................... 17

A Treatise on Irresistible Grace ........................................... 23

The Pillar and Ground of the Truth ................................... 51

A Sensible Demonstration of the Deity ........................... 69

Exact Walking ....................................................................... 89

Samuel's Support for Sorrowful Sinners ....................... 109

The New Life ...................................................................... 125

Other Works Published by Puritan Publications ....... 144

# Meet John Preston
### Edited by C. Matthew McMahon

John Preston, D.D. (1587-1628), a Puritan religious leader, was the son of Thomas Preston, a farmer. He was born in Upper Heyford in the parish of Bugbrook, Northamptonshire, and was baptized at Bugbrook church on October 27, 1587. His mother's maiden name was Alice Marsh. Her maternal uncle, Creswell, who was the mayor of Northampton, adopted Preston due to his wealth and lack of children. Creswell placed Preston in the Northampton grammar school and later with a Bedfordshire clergyman named Guest for Greek lessons. Preston enrolled as a sizar at King's College, Cambridge, on July 5, 1604, under the tutorship of Busse, who became master of Eton in 1606. King's College was renowned for music studies; Preston attempted to learn the lute, regarded as the noblest but most difficult instrument, but made little progress. In 1606, he transferred to Queens' College and was tutored by Oliver Bowles, B.D.

Creswell had left Preston some landed property, leading him to consider a diplomatic career. He planned to spend time in Paris through arrangements with a merchant, but this fell through after the merchant's death. Preston then focused on philosophy, encouraged by Porter, who succeeded Bowles as his tutor. In 1609, Preston, who had graduated with a B.A. in 1607, was selected as a fellow of Queens' College through the influence of Porter and Tyndal, master of Queens and dean of Ely. Afterward, he shifted his focus to medicine, gaining practical experience under a renowned physician in Kent and studying astrology, which was then associated with medical practice.

Around 1611, the same year he aimed to obtain an M.A., Preston heard a sermon by John Cotton (1585–1652) at St. Mary's. This sermon, which was more plain and evangelical than Cotton's usual elegant style, disappointed the audience but profoundly impacted Preston. After the sermon, Preston visited Cotton, beginning a close religious friendship that significantly influenced both of their lives. Preston then dedicated himself to studying scholastic theology, focusing on Aquinas, and also mastering the works of Duns Scotus and Ockham. This shift in focus marked a turning point, as he had previously aspired to philosophy. The deep impact of the word of God on him led to a shift in his aspirations, turning him towards a life of Christian piety and towards the ministry, a field he had previously looked down upon.

Preston played a crucial role in the election of John Davenant as master of Queens' College in 1614, succeeding Tyndal. When Tyndal died, Preston quickly traveled to London to gain support from Robert Carr, Earl of Somerset, for Davenant's election, successfully concluding the election before George Montaigne, who later became the archbishop of York, became aware of the vacancy.

During King James I's visit to Cambridge in March 1615, Preston distinguished himself as a debater. He was initially chosen as the "answerer" in a philosophy debate but ended up being the "first opponent." His debate on whether dogs could make syllogisms, a position he argued in favor of, amused King James, who shared a story about a dog, leading to Preston gaining favor at court. Sir Fulke Greville, first lord Brooke, became a supporter of Preston, although by this time, Preston had shifted his ambitions towards the ministry and was studying modern theology, particularly Calvin's works.

Preston's distance from court favor and an incident during King James' second visit to Cambridge, where he opposed his pupil Morgan playing a woman's part in a play called "Ignoramus," raised suspicions about his Puritan leanings. This strictness increased his reputation as a tutor among Puritan parents. Despite his growing reputation, Preston suffered from health issues, including insomnia. He sought advice from William Butler of Clare Hall, a successful empiric, who advised him to use tobacco, which Preston found helpful.

Preston engaged in public debates with several learned Arminian heretics and played a key role in two public disputations organized by the Earl of Warwick at York-house. The first debate was between Bishop Buckridge and Dr. White against Bishop Morton and Dr. Preston. The Earl of Pembroke noted that no one left the debate with changed opinions. The second debate involved Dr. White and Mr. Montague against Bishop Morton and Dr. Preston, where Preston's expertise and debating skills were particularly evident.

Preston, having been ordained, became dean and catechist of Queens' College. He began a series of sermons intended to form *a body of divinity*. When his college chapel became crowded with people from outside the college, an order was issued to limit attendance to college members. Preston then started an afternoon lecture at St. Botolph's, leading to a conflict with Newcome, the commissary to the chancellor of Ely. This conflict, which once resulted in the omission of common prayer to make time for Preston's sermon, led Newcome to accuse Preston of nonconformity. However, Preston managed to acquit himself in a sermon at St. Botolph's, silencing complaints. He was later invited to preach before King James at Finchingbrook, near Royston, Cambridgeshire, where

James approved his argument against the Arminians. James might have been less favorable had he known Preston was against the Spanish match, a position circulated secretly among House of Lords members. Preston was proposed as a royal chaplain by James Hamilton, second marquis of Hamilton, but James considered this premature.

Preston's relative, Sir Ralph Freeman, suggested to George Villiers, first duke of Buckingham, that promoting Preston could win Puritan support. Through Buckingham's influence, Preston became chaplain-in-ordinary to Prince Charles. He took his B.D. degree in 1620. When Davenant was elected to the see of Salisbury in 1621, Preston hoped to succeed him as Margaret professor of divinity. He planned a trip to Dutch universities to refresh his Latin, obtaining a license for travel and disguising the trip as a visit to Sir Richard Sandys in Kent and possibly to drink Tunbridge waters. From the Kentish coast, he secretly traveled to Rotterdam, dressed in layman's clothes. In Holland, he mingled with both Catholics and Protestants. Upon his return, he feigned surprise at rumors of his travels abroad. However, Williams, the lord keeper, had been monitoring his movements through a spy.

In February 1622, John Donne resigned from Lincoln's Inn, and Preston was elected as his successor. A new chapel, built to accommodate the large numbers attracted by Preston's preaching, was completed soon after his appointment. Preston's influence led to an invitation to become master of Emmanuel College, succeeding Laurence Chaderton. Chaderton, who admired Preston, hesitated to resign, fearing an Arminian replacement. Buckingham assured Chaderton of the king and prince's wish for Preston to succeed him and offered financial support. Chaderton resigned, and Preston was elected master of Emmanuel College in a secretive process. He found ways to evade the statutes limiting the master's absence, justifying his frequent absences for college business and "violent detention." However, he insisted on the rule that fellowships must be vacated. In 1623, Preston was made D.D. by royal mandate, possibly in preparation for accompanying Arthur Chichester on an embassy to Germany, though there is some confusion about this.

  Preston sought opportunities to preach in Cambridge and was proposed for a vacant lectureship at Trinity Church in 1624. King James I, preferring to keep Preston out of a Cambridge pulpit, offered him other positions, but Preston, with the support of local residents, secured the lectureship. He was with Prince Charles at Theobalds when King James I died in 1625 and accompanied Charles and Buckingham to Whitehall for Charles's proclamation as king. Preston seemed poised for significant political influence, securing a preaching license for Arthur Hildersam, but found his plans thwarted by Laud. He closed his college due to plague fears and traveled to consult Davenant at Salisbury about Richard Montagu's "Appello Cæsarem."

He also visited Plymouth, where Charles and Buckingham were, and defended Buckingham following the Rochelle disaster. Buckingham considered nominating Preston as lord keeper, but Thomas Coventry was eventually chosen.

Preston, however, was unable to convince the Puritans to support Buckingham, whom they deeply distrusted. Preston's friends emphasized the need for a conference to discuss Montagu's books and nominated John Buckeridge, bishop of Rochester, and Francis White, then dean of Carlisle, to represent one side. The other side was represented by Thomas Morton, then bishop of Coventry and Lichfield, and Preston. Buckingham, while privately asking Preston to decline participating in the conference, let others know of his influence over Preston. The conference took place in February 1626 at York House. Preston initially refused to participate but attended as an observer after it started. A second conference occurred later that month, with Preston playing a prominent role against Montagu and White.

Buckingham was elected chancellor of Cambridge University on June 1, 1626. Unlike Joseph Mead and others, Preston did not oppose this election. However, feeling his position at the university was unstable, he considered Lincoln's Inn as a potential refuge and even contemplated moving to Basle if necessary. A private letter from Preston, suggesting a strategy against Buckingham, accidentally ended up in

Buckingham's possession. As Preston's influence at court declined, the fellows of Emmanuel College petitioned the king to repeal the statute limiting their fellowships' tenure, a move supported by Buckingham. Preston had the backing of Sir Henry Mildmay, the founder's grandson. Eventually, a compromise was reached where Charles suspended the statute (May 5, 1627) until six new livings of 100£ a year were attached to the college. Buckingham was then occupied with his unsuccessful expedition to the *Isle of Ré* in June 1627. In November, Preston preached a sermon at Whitehall, seen as prophetic when news of Buckingham's defeat arrived the following Wednesday. He was not allowed to preach again, but felt he had achieved a moral victory for his cause.

Dr. Preston's robust health deteriorated due to intense study and constant preaching. He measured his life not by its length *but by how he lived*. During his final illness, wishing to die among his old friends, he went to his birthplace. After settling his worldly affairs and revising his will, he entrusted himself to God's care. As he felt death approaching, he expressed his readiness to join God and the saints, saying, "I shall not change my company; for I shall still converse with God and saints." On his last day, learning it was the Lord's Day, he remarked, "A fit day to be sacrificed on! I have accompanied saints on earth: now I shall accompany angels in heaven. My dissolution is at hand. Let me go to my home, and to Jesus Christ, who hath bought me with his precious blood." He later added, "I feel death coming to my heart. My pain shall now be turned into joy," before dying July, 1628, at the age of only forty-one. His funeral, held in Fausley church, drew a vast crowd, with the venerable Mr. Dod delivering the sermon. Fuller, listing him among Queen's College's learned writers, described him as judicious, serious, master of his emotions, an excellent preacher, a notable debater, and a skilled politician.

A portrait of him is featured in his "New Covenant," published in 1629. As described by Ball, Preston had a strong, well-proportioned body, a pleasant face, and lively eyes. He was unmarried. His will provided for his mother and brothers, established scholarships at Emmanuel College, and bequeathed his books and furniture to Thomas Ball, his favored pupil and detailed biographer.

Preston's early interest in diplomacy reflected his character, which Fuller characterized as that of a "perfect politician," adept at strategic thinking. He had significant self-control, kept his thoughts private, and was unaffected by external criticism. Ball seems to have been the only person to whom Preston openly expressed his thoughts, revealing a cautious and reserved nature. Preston was deeply committed to promoting Calvinistic theology, found in his posthumous works (edited by Richard Sibbes, John Davenport, Thomas Ball, and partly by Thomas Goodwin, D.D.) serving as a comprehensive resource for Calvinism.

*(Taken in part from the National Dictionary of biography, Oxford, 1896)*

*Sources include:*

*The Life of Preston*, by Thomas Ball, written in 1628, several times printed in an abridged form by Samuel Clarke, the martyrologist (whose last edition is in his Lives of Thirty-two English Divines, 1677, pp. 75 sq.), is full and graphic; the chronological arrangement is sometimes confused (see also Clarke's *Life of John Cotton* in the same collection, p. 219); it was edited in 1885 by E. W. Harcourt, esq., from the original manuscript at Nuneham. Fuller's *Church History*, 1655, xi. 119, 126, 131; Fuller's *Worthies*, 1662 (Northamptonshire), p. 291; Burnet's History of his Own Time, 1724, i. 19; Granger's *Biographical Hist. of England*, 1779, ii. 174, sq.; Middleton's *Biographia Evangelica*, 1780, ii. 406 sq.; Brook's *Lives of the Puritans*, 1813, ii. 356 sq.; Neal's *Hist. of the Puritans* (Toulmin), 1822, ii. 124 sq.; Heywood and Wright's *Cambridge University Transactions*, 1854, ii. 312 sq.; extracts from the *University Register, Cambridge*, per the master of Emmanuel, and from the burial register at Fawsley, per the Rev. P. W. Story.

*His works are:*

1. "The Saints Daily Exercise; or a ... Treatise of Prayer," etc., 3rd edit. 1629, 4to (on 1 Thess. v. 17).

2. "The New Covenant ... 14 Sermons on Genesis, 17:1, 2," etc., 1629, 4to.
3. "Four Sermons," etc., 1630, 4to (on Eccles. 9:1, 2, 11, 12).
4. "Five Sermons ... before his Majestie," etc., 1630, 4to (on 1 John 5:15; Isaiah, 64:4; Eph. 5:15; 1 Tim. 3:15; 1 Sam. 12:20–22).
5. "The Breastplate of Faith and Love," etc. 1630, 4to (eighteen sermons, on Rev. 1:17; 1 Thess. 1:3; Gal. 5:6).
6. "The Doctrine of the Saints Infirmities," etc., Amsterdam [1630?], 12mo (on 2 Chron. 20:18–20).
7. "Life Eternal; or a...Treatise...of the Divine...Attributes in 17 Sermons," etc. 1631, 4to.
8. "The Law Out Lawed," etc. Edinburgh, 1631, 4to (on Rom. vi. 14).
9. "An Elegant ... Description of Spiritual Life and Death," etc., 1632, 4to.
10. "The Deformed Form of a Formal Profession," etc., Edinburgh, 1632, 4to (on 2 Tim. 3:5); London, 1641, 4to.
11. "Sins Overthrow; or a...Treatise of Mortification," etc., 2nd edit. 1633, 4to (on Col. 3:5).
12. "Four...Treatises," etc. 1633, 4to (includes 1. "A Remedy against Covetousnes," on Col. 3:5; 2. "An Elegant and Lively Description of Spiritual Life and Death," on John 5:25; 3. "The Doctrine of Self-denial," on Luke 9:23, preached at Lincoln's Inn; 4. "Three Sermons upon the Sacrament," on 1 John 5:14).
13. "The Saints Qualification," etc., 3rd edit. 1634, 4to (ten sermons on Humiliation, nine of them on Rom. 1:18, the tenth preached before the House of Commons

on Num. 25:10, 11; nine sermons on Sanctification, on 1 Cor. 5:17; three on communion with Christ in the Sacrament, on 1 Cor. 10:16).

14. "A Liveles Life; or Man's Spiritual Death," etc., 3rd edit. 1635, 4to (on Eph. 2:1–3).

15. "A Sermon preached at Lincolnes-Inne," etc., 1635, 4to (on Gen. 22:14).

16. "Remains of ... John Preston," 2nd edit. 1637, 4to (includes 1. "Judas his Repentance," on Matt. 27:3–5; 2. "The Saints Spiritual Strength," on Eph. 3:16; 3. "Paul's Conversion," on Acts 9:6).

17. "The Golden Scepter...Three Treatises," etc., 1638, 4to.

18. "Mount Ebal...Treatise of the Divine Love," etc., 1638, 4to (five sermons on 1 Cor. 16:22).

19. "The Saints Submission," etc., 1638, 12mo.

20. "The Fullness of Christ," etc., 1640, 4to (on John 1:16).

21. "The Christian Freedom," etc. 1641, 4to (on Rom. 6:14).

22. "De Irresistibilitate Gratiæ Convertentis. Thesis habita in Scholis Publicis Academiæ Cantabrigiensis ... Ex ipsius manuscripto," etc. 1643, 16mo; in English, "The Position of John Preston...Concerning the Irresistiblenesse of Converting Grace," etc. 1654, 4to.

23. "Riches of Mercy," etc., 1658, 4to.

24. "Prayers," etc., 24mo; this last is in the list of works prefixed to "The Position." An "Abridgment" of six of Preston's works by William Jemmat was published in 1648, 12mo. With his sermons are sometimes

erroneously catalogued some funeral sermons (1615–19) by John Preston, vicar of East Ogwell, Devonshire.

# Introduction

By C. Matthew McMahon, Ph.D., Th.D.

The doctrine of *the Perseverance of the Saints* is a cornerstone to Christian assurance. All the letters of TULIP stand or fall together, regardless of how inconsistent some might be in understanding those five points of the doctrine of grace. In this work, John Preston takes to task the false teachings of the heretic James Arminius, and demonstrates the error that people can hold *themselves* in God's grace, or they can *work* to an end of salvation *in their own strength*. Preston's treatise is a sound treatment (though not specifically exegetically shown, but implied) that rails against both Arminianism and the Roman Catholic teachings that place "works" before grace. He *theologically* covers how *Irresistible Grace* is a sweet doctrine for the truly converted, saying that it is both imparted by God and yet received by us *though* after a manner that is *irresistible*.

In his sermon on *The Pillar and Ground of Truth*, from 1 Timothy 3:15, he shows the role of the church as the truth, and its stance as a *pillar* by the grace of God. He also shows the role of the minister in safeguarding the Church of God, drawing analogies from Scripture about their care and protection. Also, magistrates are considered, likened to nurses and gardeners, responsible for nurturing the Church to safeguard the truth and to protect it from false teachings and moral corruption as those appointed by God to protect her. Biblical examples illustrate the importance of this role and the consequences of neglecting it. The Church is described as God's flock *and* the pillar of truth, requiring diligent care by ministers and adherence to God's laws and His prescriptions by members. He also highlights the responsibility of believers to maintain the integrity of their faith, while showing the importance of righteous leadership for the well-being of the Church. This message is conveyed with an acknowledgment of the blessings under a just and gracious ruler (the magistrates who aid the church in their role), urging gratitude and obedience to such leadership for the continued prosperity and righteousness of the Church.

In his sermon on Isaiah 64:4, *A Sensible Demonstration of the Deity*, he tackles the wonderful doctrine of God's existence, coupled with eyeing creation and providence *correctly*. Preston emphasizes the importance of relying on the Creator, and having foresight and discernment in recognizing and addressing impending dangers surrounding life's circumstances, knowing full well that God governs all things. Drawing from historical and biblical examples, he illustrates that wisdom lies in perceiving and taking action against threats before they materialize. He shows that it is clear, from what we see and hear every day, that God exists and performs extraordinary acts that we often do not anticipate. That, this God is the one and only God, and idols and false gods have no genuine existence. And God both punishes those who provoke Him with terrible deeds and blesses those who patiently await His intervention with great and wondrous acts. Preston warns against complacency and encourages seeking the Creator's guidance and repentance to avert potential calamities. He underscores the notion that God's judgments are inextricably linked to human behavior and that recognizing the signs of impending judgment is crucial for individual and collective well-being. Ultimately, he emphasizes the significance of heeding God's warnings and seeking His favor to avoid the dire consequences of divine displeasure.

In his sermon on Ephesians 5:15, *Exact Walking*, "Take heed that you walk therefore circumspectly (or exactly) not as fools, but as wise," Preston emphasizes the importance of walking with God with *exactness* as a manifestation of true biblical wisdom. He highlights that genuine wisdom involves having a clear understanding of the overarching purpose and direction of one's life, particularly in relation to God's decreed plan and revealed word. We are to be *precise* in this. He argues that a truly wise person not only possesses godly knowledge but also puts it into action, as prudence requires, practical implementation in *holiness of life*. He stresses the significance of considering all aspects of a situation in light of God's word, rather than fixating on one part, as this comprehensive view is essential for wise decision-making. He shows that those who walk with exactness, aligning their lives with Christ's will and word, exemplify the highest form of wisdom, which encompasses a holistic perspective, practical application, and discernment beyond surface appearances.

In Preston's sermon on 1 Sam. 12:20-22, *Samuel's Support for Sorrowful Sinners*, he emphasizes the importance of immediate repentance and returning to God after committing sin. He argues that delaying repentance allows sin to harden the heart further and exposes individuals to more sins. Preston also highlights that sins do not bring about substantial changes in the nature of God or His covenantal relationship with individuals. He also encourages people not to believe that God will reject them after they have sinned and stresses that God is willing to forgive and receive sinners who genuinely repent. Additionally, he warns against stubbornly refusing to turn to the Lord, as such refusal is deserving of condemnation. Overall, Preston's sermon underscores the significance of prompt repentance and returning to God as the most righteous action after committing sin.

In his sermon on *The New Life*, Preston explains 1 John 5:12, where the essence of life in Jesus Christ is explored in contrast to spiritual death. He emphasizes that the quality of one's life is determined by their desires and actions in Christ, drawing parallels between a life of sin and one of grace; those in Christ, and those outside of Christ. Preston highlights that engaging in religious duties alone, such as hearing the word, reading the word, and praying, is insufficient unless they stem from and lead to inner transformation by regeneration and towards holy growth. He underlines the importance of recognizing and resisting sin as a sign of spiritual life, cautioning against the danger of persisting in known sinful behaviors before the face of God. The sermon further discusses the process of awakening to one's need for Christ and the spiritual power of faith in Him, ultimately leading to *real* spiritual life.

Preston, as a prominent and capable minister, delivers compelling messages in this work, guiding believers closer to Jesus Christ. It is refreshing to see a minister underscoring the importance of unwavering commitment to true religion, though he lived over 400 years ago. His sermons and writings stand as a warning against compromising one's faith by mixing true and false religious elements together, and to walk exactly before King Jesus in the manner God requires according to Scripture. Christians ought never to dilute the true faith with human additions, Preston underscores throughout these sermons the need for unwavering commitment to God's one and only true religion. He presses us to remember that faith and doctrine are to be based on the unchanging foundation of the Word of God.

From my study, January, 2024,
C. Matthew McMahon, Ph.D., Th.D.
John 5:39, "...search the scriptures..."

www.apuritansmind.com
www.puritanpublications.com
www.gracechapeltn.com

# A Treatise on Irresistible Grace

The Position of Dr. Preston, Master of Emanuel College in Cambridge, Concerning the Irresistibleness of Converting Grace, or *Irresistible Grace*.

James Arminius says he ascribes as much to grace as any other theologian. He says that there is nothing said by others concerning the efficacy of grace that is not also affirmed by him. It seems he believes that in all his explanations of theology in this area, or how he sets forth the power of grace, he is still misreported by those that render him injurious to the grace of God, and that he attributes too much to free-will. You will find in Augustine, that Pelagius professes just as much concerning his own ideas. And yet, in the mean time it is equally true that if Arminius' opinion stands any test, all this efficacy of grace (which he often magnifies and amplifies in words) depends *on the will of man*. It depends on the will of man in regard to the virtue of its native liberty. Here Arminius says that the will of man may receive or reject this grace, use it nor not use it, render it effectual or vain. And he says that it cannot be otherwise unless we abolish the liberty of the will altogether, and destroy those properties which are inseparable from its nature.

Lest anyone suspect that I blame him falsely with the above opinion, or say that it is simply not his own, let his words be read. They are found in a Treatise entitled *Decl. Sent. Armm.* (on page 181), and they are these, "Grace (says Arminius) is so described in Scripture, so that it may be resisted and received in vain. Man may hinder his assent to it, and deny cooperating with it. Therefore an "irresistible power and working is not to be attributed to grace." Now, if Arminius in these words does not pull down what he seemed to build in the former, you be the judge.

I know the Arminians cavil about the word *irresistible*, used by Calvin, and others of our Divines, and cry out that by this opinion of ours men are turned into puppets, acting not at all in the work of conversion. They are as stones, acted and moved by another. They say that we believe that men themselves do not believe, but God in man repents and believes for them.

But you shall easily see how falsely these things are charged on us, and how truly we say that Arminius detracts more from the grace of God than the Jesuits. If you will give me leave faithfully to set down their opinions, and briefly to compare them together, you will see the truth. In these four things shall my discourse consist: First, I will repeat the opinion of our Adversaries. Second, I will explain our own opinion on the matter. Thirdly, I will add reasons for the confirmation of our opinion. And fourthly, I will answer the objections, at least, one or two chief objections where our opinion is opposed.

As to the first, some Jesuits affirm, that the means of sufficient grace is given to all, even reprobates, but effectual grace, which shall certainly and infallibly attain its end, is given only to the elect. If we ask them where they place the efficacy of this grace, they answer, not in a physical determination of the will, but in a moral persuasion. According to them it is not of any kind, but congruous, as they call it: *i.e.* a persuasion offered with such circumstances of place, person, and time, that God, who from everlasting knows all the inclinations of the will, foresees the will shall certainly and infallibly yield to it. Therefore they distinguish between the "sufficient" and "effectual" grace; *i.e.* those who God has chosen to life by virtue of that absolute Decree He intends to offer to them. This is not only a sufficient persuasion, but a fit time, when He knows that the person called in this way, will undoubtedly obey the call of God. But those whom He has not chosen, to them He also offers a persuasion that is sufficient, but not at a time so fit, and when He foresees that they will not obey the divine calling.

From the above we gather that this is the opinion of the Jesuits:

1. That effectual vocation follows, and not precedes, the decree of election, and consequently, that the decree is absolute, not conditional.

2. That the same and equal grace is not granted to the converted and unconverted. The grace given to the elect is always more effectual. This is not in respect of

itself, but in respect of its "suitableness" which it has to the will of the man to be converted.

    3. That all to be converted shall be certainly and infallibly converted, and that only by the power of converting grace. Others just as certain, and infallibly, shall not be converted; not only because they will not, but in regard of the defect of congruity in the grace offered. They say that this kind of "grace" (its substance) is sufficient to help men possibly be converted (if those men "will"). But concerning the circumstances, it is not sufficient because it is not offered at a suitable time. For another Suarez says, "Moral persuasion, though abundant, is not sufficient." A physical or real determination is too much, to it take away liberty, but the whole efficacy of grace consists in a certainty, hardship and convenience.

    The Arminians seem to assert that the beginning, progress, and perfection of every good work is to be attributed to grace so that no man (without preventing, accompanying, and following grace) is able to think, will, or act anything that is good. But they also say this happens when men are pleased to do it, and that all this is done after a manner resistible. This leaves it in the power of the will to use or not to use that grace towards true conversion. It is apparent, that they do not heartily and really attribute these things to grace, but only do this in pretense. This will easily appear by a distinct explanation of the opinions of the Arminians.

1. First, they grant that *Divine Grace* irresistibly illuminates the understanding.

2. Second, that the affections also are excited and renewed by the same grace *irresistibly*.

3. Third, that the will is also so much stirred up by assisting grace that it is not disentangled, whereas before it was encumbered; now it is freed, whereas it was before bound; now it is awakened, whereas before it was asleep. But the Arminians utterly deny that the will is renewed by God and by a real operation inclined to good. They deny that any quality, or habit of holiness, is infused into the will by virtue of which it is inclined more to good works than to evil. They deny this because if any of this were granted, the natural liberty of the will (as they suppose) would be destroyed. Another, in this liberty they hold it essential that the will be free to act, or not to act, when all things required to its acting are in being. Let their very words be seen,[1] "Into the Mind (they say) is infused, as a habit of knowledge, into the affections holiness is infused, as hope or fear, *etc*. But such an infusion cannot be made into the will, because of its nature: freedom to will good or evil. Hence (as they say), first, there is a moral persuasion stirred up in the understanding, but by the help of preventing grace. Secondly, to this persuasion the will may assent, but by the help of concomitant grace. And thirdly, this assent may be produced into act, but by virtue of subsequent

---

[1] *The Confer. At Hague*, page 298.

grace." But to all this they diligently apply this caution: although the will can do none of these things without the help of grace, yet it is in the power of the will to resist this grace, to put it by, to neglect it or cast it away, if it pleases. Neither can it be otherwise (they say) if the natural properties of the will be preserved. Another is the idea surrounding the question explained by Joannes Arnoldus in *Against Bogerman*, (page 263); "allowing all those which God uses in working our conversion, yet conversion itself does so far remain in our power, that we may not be converted."

This opinion being asserted, the Arminians are constrained to defend more falsely these positions than those of the Jesuits. Here are the differences:

1. They defend a conditional decree grounded on the prescience of faith. The will, supposing it receives all kinds of actions from God toward it, may convert or not convert, believe or not believe. It is necessary that God first foresee who will believe, and whom not before He can choose some to life, and appoint others to wrath. But the Jesuits hold the decree to be absolute, and faith to be an effect or fruit following thereon.[2]

2. The Jesuits grant that more grace, as to how it is dispensed, is bestowed on those who are converted, than on those who are not. The Arminians deny this and teach the opposite: that more grace (as to the manner) is

---

[2] As you will see, the Jesuits are better theologians than the Arminians. -Ed.

often conferred on the unconverted than the converted being "prevenient."

3. Here also the Arminians ordinarily cast the principle of conversion, in part, on the will of man (whatever they profess in words to the contrary), whereas the Jesuits attribute it wholly to the good pleasure and will of God.

4. Here also the Arminians hold that converting and quickening grace is not peculiar to converted chosen ones, but to also be common to others. But the Jesuits confess, that congruous or suitable vocation (in which they place the efficacy of grace) is peculiar to the elect.

5. The Jesuits judge that all those whom the Holy Ghost intended to convert are certainly and infallibly converted. The Arminians utterly deny it, where they are commonly so bold as to say, that the Holy Ghost may be resisted, even then when He works on a man with the intention of his conversion.

These things being premised, I will now briefly lay down what our opinion is. But that our judgment may be thoroughly understood, we must know that the conversion of a man is perfected in these four degrees:

1. God infuses into the whole soul, and also in the will, a habit or quality of holiness, renewing it, and making it good though it was evil, and willing though it was unwilling. This means that which belongs to the nature of the will is persevered entirely, but that which was corrupt is restricted.

2. From this quality infused the are certain imperfect inclinations, that arise in the will, perverting the notice of reason, like to those which the Schoolmen call the very first motions of the heart. By these the will does not completely and effectually will that which his good, but is only initially and incompletely inclined to those good works which please God. From here such acts may be called, not so much willing, as "wishing" and "wouldings."

3. Those inclinations are presented as an object to the understanding. The understanding weighs them, debates them, takes counsel about them, and at length, when it has by its ultimate and conclusive dictates confirmed them, propounds them to the will to be chosen.

4. After those initial inclinations arising from infused grace have passed the censure of the understanding and are accepted by the preceding judgment, then at length the will puts forth a complete and effectual willingness. From this willingness conversion immediately follows, or rather that very willing conversion of a man to God.

In these four things is the conversion of a man accomplished: 1) Here first the reception of the grace infused is indeed irresistible, but neither free nor voluntary. The will is merely passive in being revived, and therefore does not exercise its "freedom." 2) Secondly, the inclination arising or flowing from grace is irresistible, for it proceeds from the will. It is formed and endued with grace, not in a moral but a physical way that is, not in a way or persuasion, but real operation. It is voluntary, for it is produced by the will in an active way. But it is not free, because one of the requisites to freedom, which is the foregoing judgment of the understanding is not available. 3) The judgment of the understanding, concerning this initial and imperfect inclination, is resistible. The understanding being enlightened by divine grace, irresistibly and infallibly approves this inclination. Here it is as far from being free as the understanding is capable of freedom. 4) Fourthly, when the understanding has put forth its last and conclusive dictate, then the will (as I said) puts forth a complete and executive willing. This is actual conversion to God. This willing is both irresistible and free, and so conversion itself is both free and irresistible. It is irresistible for two reasons: 1] because it necessarily follows the real inclination of the will preceding, and the last dictate of the understanding, approving and confirming it. It is also most properly free, because it has those things that are required for having a form of liberty. The will should be seen here as not passive, but active. 2] It is not brought forth, but in the way of moral persuasion, that is, not without the preceding judgment of the understanding, weighing on each part what is best to be done. Every active and complete willing which has had such a deliberation and determination of the understanding concerning an object offered going before it, must be called truly and properly free. For that definition of freedom where that is said to be free, which supposing all things requisite to action, may either said to be free. This supposing all things requisite to action may either act or not. It is a definition settled only in the minds of the Jesuits, and does not have a foundation among the Fathers, nor the ancient philosophers, nor even among the ancient schoolmen, whom yet Suarez endeavors to take parts of their words to maintain his own opinion.

So you have the opinion, according to which a man is converted irresistibly but also freely. Hopefully you may more fully understand these axioms follow from it and are contrary to those Jesuits and Arminians.

1. We do not say that free will, or the faculty of the will, according to spiritual things, is half alive and half dead, as the Arminians would have it.[3] It is not like the power of moving residing in a person who is shut up in a dark place, as the Papists say. We hold, that the faculty of the will, as it respects a truly spiritual good, is wholly extinct, as the power of life in a dead man, or motion in a slain man, or of sight in him whose eyes are put out.

2. They also defend that the will is only stirred up by a moral or assisting grace, knocking at the door of it, and admonishing it; not that it is changed by habitual grace, healing and renewing it. These are their words, "There is no reason why moral grace that is morally

---

[3] *Confer. Hag.* page 300.

persuading, may not make a natural man spiritual." But we suppose that the will is quickened and renewed by the infusion of habitual grace, that is, of a new quality imprinted on the will, which is as an inward principle enlivening and changing the will. From here all good inclination and operation proceeds.

3. They hold, that the will is otherwise concerned in conversion, than in any active way. We maintain, that the will in the first act of conversion is partly passive and partly active, that is first passive, then active. It does not work together with God partly by a natural ability, and partly by a supernatural strength, received from grace, passing by a virtue of a power that is supernatural, which is conferred by infused and quickening grace. According to Augustine, "to will, is of ourselves, but to will well, both partly and wholly, is of grace."

4. The Arminians think that the quickening grace of the Spirit, and whatsoever else on God's part is required to the conversion of a man is communicated as well as to the reprobate, as to the elect. They believe this is done with the intention of their salvation, otherwise God should deal deceitfully and hypocritical with them when He offers the Word to them. Let their own words be read.[4] But we hold, that the quickening grace of God, which is fit for the healing and renewing of the will, is peculiar to the elect and is imparted to them by virtue of

---

[4] *Coll. Hag.* page 308.

the divine decree. The end of this is that they might be saved. But this is denied to others, and that our God has not determined to save them.

5. They say that the will stirred up by quickening grace, may act or not act, turn to God or not. If this were not the case, they say, it would not be free. They hold liberty to stand in this, that granting all things required, or all the actings of God, the will may act or not. This is seen in the argumentation between Corvinus and Tilenus, (page 337). So they say that grace does not so furnish the will with strength, but that it always remains in the power of the will to use it or not use it. We on the contrary, say, that the will cannot resist or withstand the real motion proceeding from grace, nor the divine persuasion offered to it by an enlightened understanding, but necessarily follows the guidance of God. As Saint Augustine said, "free will cannot resist God in the word of salvation."

6. They say that the will excited by grace properly works together with God is a coordinate joint cause, a partial concomitant cause, and has such an influence into the effect that if it is withheld, the effect in way can follow. We on the contrary, say, that the will does indeed cooperate, but as a *cause*. The will is a subordinate effect, a reflex act, and wholly subject to the dominion of God as the principal agent. It cannot properly be called a coworker, but rather it acts as it is acted, moves as it is moved, and being made fit, it turns to God. Another, in that way alone, it turns itself to God.

7. They deferred that God cannot convert us in an irresistible way unless we are turned into sticks and blocks of wood. Being driven with a continual motion, we do not act anything at all, but that God is all in us. However, we say that sticks, blocks of wood or stones have no power to act at all. They are acted upon completely. Men are free agents, and therefore have a power by virtue of which they act, being acted by God, and therefore may be said truly to act, and turn themselves to God. The well-being of their hearts changed from evil to good, and of unwilling made willing. This has in itself an inward principle of willing well. From here the dominion of its own act is seen where it turns to God; the ability to "turning" now properly given to it by God. The grace of God is the principle by which this happens, and yet the will of man is the principle that works it out practically. In like manner, although God be the first and total efficient cause of conversion, yet the will is the next efficient cause, and total also in the kind of second causes, therefore as the effects are wont to be attributed to second and created causes, although they act by virtue of the first cause, so conversion is more properly to be attributed to the will, although it act wholly in the strength of God and converting grace.

8. Lastly, they deny that the irresistibleness of divine grace, and the liberty of man's will, can stand together. But we say, that conversion is irresistible, but

also free. Yet, we are careful to distinguish how grace is irresistible.

1. There is one kind of irresistibleness whereby regenerating grace infused from God is received by the will. This irresistibleness of reception, we confess, cannot stand with liberty.

2. There is another kind, whereby the inclination putting on to spiritual good flows from, after a physical or real manner, the will fashioned by grace. This motion, we say, comes from the will irresistibly and voluntarily, but not freely.

3. There is an irresistibleness where the will assents to this physical motion proceeding from the grace, as also to the persuasion of the understanding approving of it. It does this necessarily or certainly. This kind of irresistibleness, we say, may very well stand with liberty, because it comprehends in itself those two things in which liberty stands: 1) that the will in putting forth this last act of willing is active and not passive; 2) because the moral persuasion or judgment of the understanding, thinking that the conversion propounded, (either the taking or refusing the object offered is in the power of man) has gone before. For we hold that whatsoever is done in the act of conversion, either by a mere reception, or by a physical (or powerful) determination, is not free. But that every willing is only so far free as it is produced in an36ardshe way and flows from a reasonable persuasion. On this ground, that reason lies indifferent to things opposite; *i.e.* reason only

is the root and foundation of all liberty. From here it follows that every act of the will into which reason has its influence is most free.

Hopefully you now see what our opinion is through this lengthy opening. We took such a long time to explain this because the explication of it is the chief confirmation and the confutation of the contrary. Besides, it is a very difficult thing to express what the Arminians hide in this dispute because they cover and wrap up their opinion in so many doubtful and suspicious words.

We still have certain arguments to set forth by which our opinion is so to be confirmed. I will be brief in them. Two things are to be proved: 1) that qualities or habits may be infused into the will. The Arminians deny this because they suppose that such an infusion utterly destroys and takes away the nature and liberty of the will. And 2) that this habitual and quickening grace, being infused in this way, is that which God uses to convert the soul, and is irresistible to any man's efforts to the contrary. Here are the following arguments for this:

Argument 1: that there is such an infusion of grace renewing and healing the will, inclining and determining it to one of the two opposites in the act of conversion. All good divines universally accept this: that there is in the will an habitual aversion from God, and a habitual turning to sensible and carnal things. But this habitual corruption of nature cannot be healed by the sole help of grace simply exciting it. Corporeal and spiritual diseases are not cured except by some kind of medicine. Therefore, in the same way, habitual corruption cannot be changed but by a habitual quality imprinted on the will. *Prop.* Therefore says right, "The inward sense is not opened to do spiritual things, until the foundations of faith, and fervor of love is planted in the heart."[5]

Argument 2: Unless it is granted that such a habitual grace is infused into the will, by which it is inclined to good after a physical manner, there will be found no formal principle in man from where good acts may be produced. Man cannot see physical things unless he first has eyes. He cannot hear unless he has ears. In spiritual things no man sees unless God has first given him eyes to see, nor does he hear unless he has given him ears to hear. By the same reason no man can turn himself to God unless he has a new heart. A new heart is a new will to turn and love God. What does the Scripture mean that says, "An evil tree bringeth forth evil fruit, a good tree bringeth froth good fruit?" But that we should understand is that the will must first be made good before it can perform any spiritual work. This must necessarily be done, not by an exciting or persuading grace, but by a healing and regenerating grace.

Argument 3: It is not that the mere help of exciting grace could raise the will, deformed by habitual

---

[5] Preston does not give us any inclination who "Prop" is. -Ed.

corruption, to the acting out of spiritual acts. This would be contrary to the sweetness of divine Providence, which is acknowledged by all divines. For God does not sweetly woo or wish the will work act spiritually, but in a forced way hurries it on to its work, which its own inclination is averse from. It is therefore better to understand this as a certain habitual propension to spiritual good, which it may perform. But this is not by virtue of some kind of "exciting grace," but from the infusion of *habitual grace*.

Argument 4: Every orthodox scholar confesses that the unrenewed will has no principle in it that is truly spiritual. And yet Arminians will not deny that this act of turning to God is truly spiritual and supernatural. But I cannot fathom how they can possibly say that the will is only excited by motioning grace and not changed by regenerating grace. If this were the case then man should be placed in the rank of supernatural agents.

Argument 5: I ask, "what is it that makes a man truly holy and godly, not simply acts good and godly? As the Philosopher says, "Acts do not demonstrate the subject to be such." It must therefore be some habit, by virtue of which a man is called godly and holy. But that habit is not placed in the irrational part of the soul, for that is not properly capable of virtue or vice, but only by participation as the rational part of the soul acts upon it. But if it must be placed in the rational part, it must not be in the understanding, for no man is good or evil, only because he understands good and evil things (as

Aquinas very well observes). But one is called a good or evil man, because he wills those things which are good and evil.[6] It remains therefore, that the habit of holiness cannot be placed anywhere but in the will as being the subject most properly capable, both of habitual holiness, as also of habitual corruption and rebellion, which is contrary to it.

Argument 6. If the will is indifferent in itself, and equally inclined into either part, where is that facility and promptitude in working? For as by evil actions the will contracts a stain where it is habitually disposed to evil, so by good actions the soul is touched with better tint, where it is habitually inclined to good and that setting aside the operation of moving and exciting grace.

Argument 7. All good divines do not acknowledge that charity or the love of God is not just a mere act but also a permanent habit. That habit itself does not have understanding, because it is an affection, not in the sensitive appetite, which cannot be raised to a spiritual love. It remains that it is peculiar to the will and so the will to be most properly capable of habits of habitual grace.

Argument 8. Lastly, how absurd is it to grant the whole man to be dead in sin, so that it can no way to reach to any good truly spiritual, and at the same time

---

[6] Preston is not denying *Total Depravity* here, something he has been upholding. Rather, he is simply demonstrating the manner in which the will, as a will, works for good or evil, and is not neutral – something he will call "void". -Ed

defend that the will, which is the very leader of the soul, the driver of all faculties, the lady and Queen of human acts, and that principle which imparts spiritual good or evil, to all actions which men perform. I think it is quite absurd to hold that his faculty was neither spiritual before the fall, nor carnal after the fall, but to be utterly void, both of the corruption brought in by the first fault, and of spiritual gifts infused in the regeneration of man.

It is very easy to overwhelm the Arminian's opinions with more absurdities, but these shall suffice. By all these things it is apparent enough that a new quality or habit of grace is infused into or impressed on the will. This is earnestly denied by the Arminians, as has been before proved by their own words.

If you really doubt that this is their opinion, then read the *Hague Conference*, (page 298), of Bertius' translation[7] where they industriously and purposefully defend the ideas that in spiritual death spiritual gifts are not separated from the will of man. Nor do they teach that they were implanted in it before death in the state of 4lardship4l (which is ridiculous). What they are contending for is the neutrality of man's free will that is inclined neither to one side or another, but acts as it sees fit in each situation (which is contradictory).

It remains now briefly to be proved that God, whether immediately or mediately, both by infused grace and moral persuasion, turns sinners to Himself in

---

[7] Or read the Works of James Arminius. -Ed.

an irresistible manner. But this caution is to be promised, that by the word *irresistibility* we do not understand any force offered to the will, which is repugnant to nature, but only an insuperable efficacy of divine grave. This inclines the will sweetly and agreeably to its own nature. And this certainly and necessarily cannot be put off by the will.

1. The truth of this opinion is manifest from this: that everywhere in Scripture the conversion and regeneration of a sinner is attributed to God alone and to His good will and pleasure. Even the least cooperation is taken away from man himself. Romans 9 is quite plain, "It is not of him that willeth, nor of him that runneth, but of God that showeth mercy…He has mercy on whom he will have mercy and whom he will he hardeneth." Who could really say that a man, at his own freedom and pleasure, allows all the actions of God requisite to conversion, still may receive the quickening grace of God in vain and make it void? This is what Arminius says. And let it be observed from these words, "That this is man's repenting, and that man's hardening, is not only attributed to God alone, but the will and endeavor of man, is utterly excluded from having any part in this business." On the contrary, "It is not," says the apostle, "of him that willeth nor of him that runneth, *etc.*" As the wheel does not run well that it may be round, but because it is first round it runs well. So a man does not therefore will or run that God might have mercy on him, and regenerate him by the quickening grace of the spirit,

but because God *first* has mercy, therefore he wills and runs in the way of righteousness.

2. The second reason is taken from the infallible connection of the effect, with the cause of conversion, with converting and quickening grace. For if this quickening grace always attains its effect, it is not offered to any but those in whom it is effectual; to the healing and regenerating of their soul. We must necessarily attribute to it a certain, prevalent and irresistible working. But it appears by many places of Scripture, that this grace always attains its end in those to whom it is communicated. John 6:37 says, "Whatsoever my Father giveth me cometh to me." Jeremiah 31:23 says, "Turn thou me and I shall be turned." From here it is gathered that to whomever the grace of conversion is infused, that man is certainly and infallibly converted. Otherwise a man could not address God in this way, "Turn me," that is, "do what Thou art wont to do by the help of Thy Spirit, and the infusion of thy Grace, and I shall be converted." For perhaps the will, in whose power it is to receive or reject grace, may make it void. The same is evident from John 6:45, "Whosoever has heard and learned of the Father cometh to me," that is, whosoever has so heard and been taught of God, that he has also received and drunk in the quickening grace of the Spirit, he has certainly come to Me. Here it appears that grace fit for the conversation of a man is never frustrated, but it attains its effects after an insuperable manner so that it can never be put off by

the will of man. This is further confirmed from the nature of grace, and that powerful manner, where God infuses it into the heart of man. For by grace is the effect of infinite power, and that man is regenerated by the same power where Christ was raised from the dead. Then God, in the imparting of it in the will of man, puts forth that almighty power which no created faculty is able to withstand or resist.

3. This argument may also be added, the grace of God is so much the efficient cause of conversion that it admits no joined and coordinate cause, although it has a subordinate cause. The will of man is not the cause of it though it is joined to it. If the will, when it is excited by assisting grace (as they call it) can resist it, then it may also assist it, withstand it, or make joint endeavor with it, to produce the same effect. If it can make it void, it may also make it effectual, and so may be a *cause* coordinate with the grace of God in bringing forth the first act of its conversion. But that God converts or regenerates men by His own and only work, excluding all coordinate causes, is so clear that it does not need to be proved. This is frequently found in Scripture: the Lord converts, the Lord gives repentance, that God circumcises, and takes away the stony heart, and gives a heart of flesh.

Lastly, that God regenerates the soul, and by His own power raises from the death of sin.

This is a strong and helpful analogy to consider: as no man can contribute anything to his own generation or resurrection, so neither to his spiritual regeneration or resurrection. God does all these things. But if man partakes in aiding God in any way these acts of power could be attributed both to God and to man. And if man has such power, and he refused to cooperate, then God's power is voided and the effect of regeneration could not follow.

I add, that of the Schoolmen is most true, that God is the cause of the whole being: that is, although God is not the efficient cause of sin (which is not a being, but rather a defect of what should be in the faculty or act) but rather a deficient will, but of every good work (of which kind our first conversion is a chief one) if it be most full of being, or if it be a whole being, as it is, of such a whole work, I say, it is necessarily that God should be the cause, for God alone is the cause of the whole being wheresoever it is found. All divines acknowledge that so far as sin itself is a being, God is the cause of it, but it is not. Wherefore although the will be the secondary and subordinate efficient cause of conversion, from where it is that the Scriptures do exhort us to turn ourselves, and circumcise our hearts, and so forth. Yet, as a coordinate cause, in no way can resist the quickening grace of God, and receive it in vain, as Arminius speaks. But I also add, although God would admit of a partner in this work, yet the will, which is wholly depraved and dead in sin, can no more cooperate with exciting and moving grace than a carcass decomposing can revive itself or put forth vital acts. But that I may conclude this reason, if it is supposed that the will may work together with the grace of God, if this opinion stands, how much more will be given to man's glory and detracted from the glory of God? Man may well boast that his will contributed so much to regeneration, that if he had not willed, it had never been produced. For someone who is admonished by another to give alms does it, he thinks he persuaded himself more than the other. In the same way the will that is only moved and admonished by assisting grace, turned *itself* to God, ascribes his conversion to himself than to divine grace. If he had not cooperated, then conversion would never have been produced. He had to consent to it, and made its persuasion effectual, otherwise he would have frustrated the power of God. How is this glorifying to God? Rather, it puffs up man's depravity.

The fourth reason is taken from this, that the decree of election (by which God determined with Himself to save some persons selected from the common mass) is absolute, and therefore necessarily and infallibly attains its effect. The decree of election is absolute, so that the Lord looked on nothing foreseen in the persons chosen, but absolutely decreed to work in them all conditions required to salvation. This is so clearly manifest from many places of Scripture, that it hardly needs any proof. We did not choose God, but He chose us, John 15. We are chosen that we might be holy, not holy that we might be chosen. He chose Jacob rather than Esau, when both were of like and equal condition,

Romans 9. Effectual vocation[8] and justifying faith are the fruits and effects of predestination not the foregoing conditions, see Romans 8. Lastly, if God's mere good pleasure is the only reason of the decree (He has mercy on whom He will and hardeneth whom he will) it necessarily follows that God has absolutely decreed to save some. To absolutely save some He bestows on them grace, faith, and holiness. Granting these things, it appears that God converts all the elect after a manner that is irresistible, because if they could resist that grace, which is fit to convert them, being also given to this end, that they might be converted, then this absolute and preemptory decree of God might be disappointed by the creature, which must not be imagined. Neither is their any ground that they should now object to the way God saves, for by the same reason, those whom God has rejected sin irresistibly. For we deny that there is the same reason of both: for although faith is the effect of predestination, yet infidelity is to the proper effect of reprobation. Faith requires a cause of itself that is efficient, and has a true and proper influence to its effect. But there is no efficient cause required to unbelief. It is deficient (because it follows on the mere defect and absence of that cause by which faith should be created in someone). In the same way, to see light outside there is a required of the sun, or some other efficient cause, a tendency to that effect; but the absence of the sun is

---

[8] *i.e.* Effectual Calling. -Ed

enough to cause darkness. In the same manner, although the sins of reprobates infallibly follows from the determinate counsel of God, who has decreed their event, yet conversion and faith follow the absolute decree of God after a much different manner. Sins follow infallibly indeed, but only by a necessity of consequence, that is, God is not at all causing or effecting sin in their heart, but only permitting. Faith and good works follow by necessity of the consequence, so God must most properly be called the Author, according to all divines. No man ever said that God permits men to believe, to become regenerate, to turn to Christ, and to do good works, but rather *caused* them to do so and to work good works. This should be granted: that faith and conversion follow the absolute decree of God by a necessity of the consequent; *i.e.* a necessity causing. I cannot see how it could be denied that it is wrought in us after an irresistible manner. For when any agent so works on the patient, then it necessarily overcomes it. It is properly said to work irresistibly. In the same way God, if He converts a sinner, that sinner is necessarily converted. He is by necessity the consequent of an irresistible conversion. The patient has no choice in this matter as such. I am at a loss as to why anyone would want to believe that grace is resistible; those who deny election, or make it depend on foreseen faith that is really the same thing, and defend that conversion can be resisted, and that it can be frustrated.

Let this be the first and last reason. If conversion is shaped after a resistible manner, as is described by those who follow Arminius, then divine election cannot be certain according to their principles, because it depends on the mutable will of man. It is described by Arminius, I dare say, as foreseen by God Himself. They suppose as the foundation of that idea that God perfectly foresees all the ways where the will may be turned aside, or inclined to good. Suppose for a second this is true. Suppose also that God foreknows all objects or circumstances, which may anyway be offered or proposed to the will. Lastly, let us also suppose that God perfectly knows how every object or circumstance is fit to move the will, and drive it this way or that way by persuasion. Yet if this is really the condition of the will, that allowing any objects, allowing any fitness in these objects or circumstances to incline the will this way or that way, it may yet, by virtue of its intrinsic liberty to act, or not act. I cannot see how God can foresee what the will certainly and infallibly will do; *i.e.* whether it will turn to God or not. Not that God, by reason of any impotency is not able to search out what the will shall endeavor, but because the thing itself is *not knowable*. For there cannot be greater certainty in the knowledge than in the object, from here we reason to overthrow their opinion: if it is certain that the will shall assent to grace offered, then it is falsely said, that the will supposing all the actions of God that are requisite, may turn itself or not. On the other side, if it is uncertain, whether the will shall resist this grace, or not, then that foreknowledge which God has of it, cannot be certain, for that which is to be known is the measure of knowledge, and therefore it is a contradiction to say that the knowledge is true and at the same time there is more certainty in the knowledge than in the thing known. As it implies a contradiction to say that the thing measured is greater or less then the measure and yet to be equal to it, although it is true that God knows all the ways according to which the will may be well or ill inclined. If the will be altogether undetermined, admitting nothing to determine it neither within itself nor without it, whether created, or uncreated, as they defend, implies a contradiction that any certain way, where it should fall out that the will should be ordered or disordered, can be determined by God himself. Out of the these things it is gathered, that if converting grace moves the will after a certain manner that may be resisted by it, God cannot infallibly foreknow who shall believe and who do not, and consequently, all election should be utterly taken away. Therefore the truth of irresistible grace remains and the doctrine of God stands secure, otherwise it would be overthrown.

 The conclusion is that converting grace is both imparted by God and received by us after a manner that is irresistible.

FINIS

# The Pillar and Ground of the Truth

"But if I tarry long, that thou mayest know how thou oughtest to behave thyself in the house of God, which is the church of the living God, the pillar and ground of the truth," (1 Tim. 3:15).

There are two main principles upon which the *entire* structure of Popery is built. First, they believe that the Church of Rome is the only universal Church. Second, they believe that the Church cannot err. This second principle leads them to a desperate situation where they cannot amend or reform anything once it's decided by the Church. These are the principles they instill in their novices and use to persuade people. When they cannot prove their specific points, they rely on this general principle that "Our Church, which cannot err, has decided it," bundling multiple beliefs together. If they cannot find scriptural support for their practices such as the invocation of saints, worshiping images, indulgences, additional sacraments, and numerous superstitious rituals, they claim that the *Church* has decided it, and its decrees are infallible, beyond questioning by "ordinary" individuals. So, they hide behind this pillar, asserting the infallibility of the Church, which cannot be scrutinized. While truth seeks the light and welcomes examination, Popery thrives in obscurity and vague generalities.

For instance, if you ask them for the basis of practices like the invocation of saints, image worship, indulgences, and additional sacraments, their response is, "The Church has decreed it, and its decrees are infallible; they are not to be questioned by inferior individuals." Therefore, if you pull down this pillar, as Samson did, the entire structure of Popery, and those relying on it, will come crashing down.

However, since they find it unlikely to build their beliefs solely on the Church's assertion, which only interprets but doesn't create the text cited by Paul, they introduce Traditions, which they call *unwritten truths*, and consider them *equally* valid as the Text. But when you ask them about these unwritten truths and how to distinguish them from counterfeits, they say only the Church can determine that, as these were entrusted to its care, and only the Church can infallibly judge which traditions are genuine and which are not. Moreover, if Scripture is ever cited against their beliefs, they argue that it's the Church of Rome's prerogative to declare which books of Scripture are canonical, what translation is authoritative, and what interpretation must be followed. In essence, they allow *themselves* to be the sole judges, and whatever we say, they shut us down with these principles: "Ours is the only Church," and "The Church can never err."

Now, of all the verses in Scripture they use to support their privilege, the one I just read is among the most important. But we need to examine if they interpret it correctly.

The Apostle writes to Timothy, saying, "I have written to you so that you may know how to behave in the house of God." It implies that the proper *order* and maintenance of the house of God are essential because it serves as the *Pillar and Ground of Truth*. In other words, this house of God is where *Truth*, which is the spiritual nourishment, is preserved and grown. If falsehood creeps into it, the spiritual nourishment becomes poisoned and leads to corruption and destruction instead of salvation. Another, the Apostle has two main objectives in this verse:

First, he distinguishes the Church by describing it as the Pillar and Ground of Truth. This is the identifying characteristic of the house of God.

Second, he specifies "in the house of God" without specifying any particular city or location. This is crucial because it prevents the misconception that Truth is permanently tied to a specific place, which goes against the Apostle's intent. In the beginning of the next chapter, the Apostle clearly states that, in later times, some will depart from the faith, embracing false teachings that forbid marriage and certain dietary restrictions.

The Papists argue that because Truth was once in Rome, it is still there. They may point to the location, but the inhabitant, which is Truth, has departed. Instead, errors have taken its place, as the Apostle foresaw when he mentioned the forbidding of marriage and dietary restrictions. They may argue that they do not forbid everyone from marrying, but they do restrict some from marrying at certain times, particularly the clergy, and this is not just a matter of convenience but of necessity and holiness.

The Papists claim that the Church is the pillar and ground of truth to the extent that all truth comes *from* the Church, and whatever comes from the Church is infallibly true and beyond error. However, this cannot be what the Apostle intended. First, there can be truths found in writings outside the Church. While a garden is the most suitable place for herbs, violets may also grow in the woods and along the roadside. So, by "Truth" here, the Apostle means divine and sacred truth, something originating from God's garden, not the wilderness.

Furthermore, errors can exist within the Church. Just as a garden is the proper place for herbs but may also contain weeds, the Church may harbor errors, just as a field may have both wheat and tares. When the Apostle says, "The Church is the pillar and ground of truth," he means that the Church must preserve and uphold the truth. It is the duty of those who claim to be part of the Church to maintain the truth, a responsibility they must fulfill. However, the mere obligation to do so does not guarantee that it will always be accomplished. It is not a valid inference to assume that something is surely done just because someone should do it. People do not always fulfill their duties or responsibilities, and they may not exercise the trust placed in them.

The Apostle speaks in general terms, stating that "The Church is the pillar and ground of truth," without specifying any particular city or country. The Church may move from one place to another, and truth goes with it. While the Church remains in a place, the fundamental truths remain, but when it relocates, the truth goes with it. If they object, claiming that a pillar is a supporting structure that cannot be moved without destroying the building, and since the Church of Rome was once the pillar and ground of truth, it remains so, the response is that the Apostle is referring to a different *kind* of pillar. He means a pillar on which proclamations and notices are hung, which can easily be separated from the building. The same applies to the word "foundation," which signifies a receptacle that can be separated from its contents. Therefore, the people of Ephesus, who stood long after the truth departed, serve as an example. The truth can be taken down and placed elsewhere, just as herbs can be transplanted from one garden to another. While the Church remained in Rome, the truth persisted, but no longer does it reside there.

The Papists' claim that the Church of Rome cannot err in matters of faith and doctrine is not supported by the Apostle's intent in this verse. God alone is infallible, and humans, including the Church, are fallible. Ignorance can lead to error, and even the most learned bishops in general councils have been ignorant of.

Secondly, considering that we have demonstrated that the judgment of the Church is not infallible in matters of faith and doctrine, we can learn not to accept things solely on trust, not to assume something is true just because *the Church* has declared it. This foundation is unreliable for building our faith; our faith should be built upon the solid rock, *which is the word of God.* It's worth noting that many aspects of Popery, such as the invocation of Saints, the worship of Images, the universal and supreme authority of the Bishop of Rome, the concept of purgatory, Popish indulgences, prayers in an unknown tongue, prayers for the dead, consecration of oil, tapers, and holy water, and various other superstitious ceremonies, cannot be found in the Bible. These practices are like hay and stubble, accumulated over time according to personal preferences until the corruption of true faith reached its peak. These controversies are all rooted either in the decrees of the Pope, unwritten traditions, the authority of the Church, or Scripture being twisted to fit their interpretations. The very essence of Popery hinges on the belief that *their* Church does not err, and if this principle is discredited, the entire system crumbles.

Thirdly, just as the Apostle here advises Timothy and all ministers to be cautious and circumspect in their conduct within the Church of God, so should all

Magistrates, both supreme and subordinate, be vigilant and cautious in their behavior within this Church of God. While Ministers are like bees that produce spiritual nourishment, Magistrates are like the hives that house and protect this spiritual nourishment. Ministers are responsible for defending the Church through preaching and teaching, while Magistrates use their authority and power to safeguard it. Ministers handle the spiritual aspects,57ardse Magistrates oversee the order and execution of religious practices. The text itself provides motivations for this.

The Church of God is like a house, and it is only fitting for its inhabitants to keep it in good repair. *Both* Ministers and Magistrates bear this responsibility. Neglecting the maintenance of the house leads to the intrusion of heresies and superstitions that corrupt the family within.

The Church of God is also likened to a flock, and good Magistrates serve as its shepherds, just as David did. If wolves enter through their negligence and harm the sheep, they will be held accountable by God, just as Laban demanded restitution from Jacob.

Moreover, the Church is described as the pillar and foundation of truth, and Magistrates are like gardeners or caretakers of this garden of truth. They must ensure that the good plants are nourished, the weeds and stones hindering growth are removed, and the protective hedge is maintained. Otherwise, the Serpents of their time may infiltrate the Garden and corrupt the minds of the faithful. Similar motivations can be found throughout Scripture, such as in Revelation 2:20, which warns against tolerating errors and their authors in the Church of God. "Notwithstanding I have a few things against thee, because thou sufferest that woman Jezebel, which calleth herself a prophetess, to teach and to seduce my servants to commit fornication, and to eat things sacrificed unto idols," (Rev. 2:20).

    Christ promised, as mentioned in John 16:13, to send His Spirit to guide believers into all truth, and in Matthew 28:20, to remain with them until the end of the world. These passages should primarily be understood as applicable to the Apostles themselves, who were infallibly led into every truth, and only secondarily to their successors, insofar as they follow in their footsteps and teachings. If we were to interpret these promises as Bellarmine, Stapleton, and other Catholic writers do, suggesting that the promise is *equally* applicable to their successors, then individual bishops and ministers would be *infallible* judges of truth and falsehood, ultimately ending all disputes in the Church, which is *not* the case. Some may argue that the promise is not intended for individual leaders but for gatherings in Synods. However, there is no indication of such a distinction in these passages. Instead, a more fitting place for such a promise is found in Matthew 18:20, where Jesus stated, "Where two or three are gathered together in my name, there am I in the midst of them." This statement applies not only to larger Councils but also to smaller gatherings of true Christians, which would make the promise of infallibility accessible to *all*.

Furthermore, some argue that without a visible, external, infallible judge to whom those unable to navigate the depths of theological controversies can turn, there would be endless disputes and no reliable means to ascertain the truth in disputed matters. While there may not be an infallible, visible, human judge, there is an invisible, infallible judge—the Holy Spirit—speaking in the Scriptures, which are referred to as *the word of God*. This judge surpasses any other in several ways. Firstly, it is readily available and accessible to people of all backgrounds, while human judges may be elusive and hard to reach. Secondly, the verdict of this judge is certain and unchangeable, unlike human judges who can be swayed. Human judges have affections, which is why there are laws among men since the law itself cannot have affections, but the lawyer does. Thirdly, if this judge is better known it can be more easily agreed upon by all. Even if we were to assume that the true Church is an infallible judge, it is easier to determine which is the true Scripture than which is the true Church, given the multitude of claimants to the latter.

While the Church continues to exist on Earth, God has not declared an end to controversies, as some may wish. In fact, 1 Corinthians 11:19 states, "For there must be also heresies among you, that they which are approved may be made manifest among you." This implies that controversies and heresies will persist to distinguish those who truly love the truth and those who do not.

If God had appointed a means within His Church to infallibly resolve controversies, a general Council, while deserving respect, is unlikely to fulfill that role. Would God appoint a means to end controversies in His Church that was unavailable for at least three hundred years, until the time of Constantine the Great? Even when he and his successors could convene councils while the Empire was undivided, the situation changed when the Empire fragmented, with different regions governed by various kings of different religions. Given the current situation, the Church cannot benefit from such councils.

So, what is the purpose and benefit of general Councils, assuming they could be convened? They serve as the best means to seek the truth, as many candles provide more light, and many eyes see more than one. In the multitude of counselors, there is health. While they are the best means to find the truth, their authority is not absolute. General Councils can err, even on essential and fundamental matters. Examples include the Councils of Ariminum and Seleucia, which erred on a fundamental point by endorsing the Arian heresy against the deity of Christ. The second Council of Ephesus and ten other councils in various cities, such as Tyre, Jerusalem, Philadelphia, Ariminum, Seleucia,

Constantinople, and Alexandria, made similar errors. Additionally, the second Council of Nice introduced the veneration of images and commanded their worship, contradicting the previous decision of the second Council of Constantinople, which had condemned such practices.

Additional examples could be provided, but these are sufficient to support the conclusion that a general Council *can err* in fundamental matters. While the universal Church of Christ, referring to His mystical body on earth and the complete number of His chosen ones, cannot err in fundamental matters (for otherwise, they might apostatize, and the gates of hell would prevail against them); the external visible body of the Church *can* err. This is because the truth of God may reside within the hearts of a group that, in a vote, cannot constitute a majority in a general Council. As a result, the decisions made in such a Council may contain fundamental errors.

From these established principles, three applications can be drawn. Firstly, since it is the accepted and endorsed doctrine of the Catholics that the Church of Rome cannot err in matters of faith and doctrine, it becomes evident that there is little hope for reconciliation between us and them, or that a consensus of opinions could ever be reached. If they were to concede anything to us, it would imply that in what they now concede, they were previously in error. This would undermine the fundamental belief in their Church's infallibility. While we can adjust our beliefs, they are firmly committed to retaining theirs without any alteration. We may be willing to compromise, but they cannot. Witness the German Interim, which was meticulously and frequently adjusted, with only a few of their doctrines omitted. Yet, it was more than Charles the Fifth could achieve to gain acceptance on either side. Another, those who believe they can reconcile us through cunning and strategy are attempting the impossible. What middle ground can be forged from materials when neither side can spare even the smallest piece of timber from their structure? They cannot do so because it would suggest that they were previously mistaken. We cannot do so because true religion is fragile; you can break it, but you cannot bend it, not even slightly. It cannot be adapted to interests and political considerations; it cannot be mixed with error, any more than oil can be mixed with water or iron and steel can be combined with clay (Daniel 2:43). As the elements, once combined in a compound body, lose their distinct forms, religions, when mixed and combined with others, lose their forms and cease to be religions in God's eyes. In 2 Kings 17:33, it is stated that the mixed people of Samaria feared the Lord and served their own gods, following the customs of the nations from which they were taken. They attempted to blend both Jewish and pagan beliefs, thinking it would satisfy both parties. But what does God say? Does He approve of this mixture? In verse 34, it is said, "Unto this day they do after the former manners, they fear not the Lord, neither do they after their statutes, or after the law or commandment which the Lord commanded." God *does not accept* His own prescribed worship when it is mixed and combined with another.

Galatians 5:1-2 advises not to become entangled again with the yoke of bondage. This means to be cautious about embracing the rites and customs of the ceremonial law, which Christians have been freed from through Christ. However, the question arises, what if circumcision, the ancient sign, is retained and joined with Christ? Is it safer to adhere to both? But Paul responds in Galatians 5:2, stating that if you are circumcised, Christ will be of no benefit to you. Furthermore, in Galatians 5:4, he says that Christ will become ineffective for you. This implies a choice between Christ and circumcision, as you cannot have both. Similarly, Isaiah 1:21-22 compares the once faithful city to a harlot, evidenced by the corruption of its silver into dross and its wine diluted with water. The presence of silver and wine is not denied, but their purity is compromised, much like how adding chaff to wheat diminishes the wheat's value.

Jeremiah 23:28 emphasizes speaking God's word faithfully, as anything added to it is considered worthless, like chaff compared to wheat. Mixing true and false religions is akin to overreaching and failing to hold onto what is intended, as illustrated by Jeroboam's mixing of truth and falsehood. He altered the place and manner of worship, not to change the worship itself but for political reasons, thinking to make religion *subordinate* to his political goals (1 Kings 12:26). This resulted in *nullifying* both religion and his family's claim to the kingdom. Similarly, Saul lost his kingdom because he *did not* fully obey God's command to destroy the Amalekites, sparing Agag and some cattle. Moses refused to compromise with the King of Egypt, insisting on taking everything belonging to the Israelites. Mordecai, obeying God's command not to make peace with Amalek, risked his safety rather than show respect to Haman, an Amalekite. Daniel, commanded to pray toward the Temple, did so even at the risk of his life.

Those with complete devotion to God will not alter or dilute their religious practices. God rejects mixed or corrupted religions. Just as a garment of mixed linen and wool was forbidden for Jews, a religion mixed with truth and falsehood is unacceptable. God detests lukewarm religions, much like the stomach rejects lukewarm water. Elijah urged the people to choose between God and Baal, not to waver between them. It is vital not to mix truth and falsehood, which God finds intolerable. Being a Papist might be due to ignorance, but consciously blending elements of it for worldly benefits *is a sin of knowledge*. A genuine belief in either Catholicism or Protestantism would lead one to adhere solely to *that* belief. Mixing beliefs for personal advantage is *unacceptable to God*. This warning is preventative, considering future temptations.

Since the Church's judgment is not infallible in matters of faith and doctrine, one should not accept beliefs merely on trust or because the Church declares them. Our faith should be based on the word of God, the rock, rather than the sandy foundation of the Church's authority. Many Catholic doctrines, such as the invocation of saints, worshipping of images, the Bishop of Rome's supremacy, purgatory, indulgences, praying in an unknown language, praying for the dead, and various superstitions, lack biblical support. These are founded on the Pope's decrees, unwritten traditions, the Church's authority, or misinterpretations of Scripture. The principle of the Church's infallibility underpins much of Catholicism. Removing this principle would cause Catholicism to collapse.

Lastly, the Apostle Paul's exhortation to Timothy, and through him to all ministers, to be careful in *their* conduct in the Church of God, *also* applies to magistrates, both supreme and subordinate. They must be cautious in their roles within the Church. Ministers may produce the 'honey' of spiritual nourishment, but magistrates provide the structure and support for this work. Ministers defend the Church with words and writings, while magistrates do so with their political authority and power. While ministers are responsible for the execution of word and sacraments, magistrates ensure an orderly and proper setting for the church. The text underscores that the Church is the house of God, and it is reasonable for its caretakers, including magistrates and ministers, to maintain and repair it. Neglecting the Church's upkeep leads to the infiltration of heresies and superstitions, which can deceive and lead astray the Church's members.

The Church of God, as described in Isaiah 49:23, is likened to a child under the care of good magistrates, who act as nurses. Just as a nurse is responsible for ensuring a child is fed healthy food and protected from dangers, magistrates are tasked with defending the Church. They must ensure it is nourished with truth rather than falsehood, as they are answerable to God, who purchased the Church with His blood (Acts 20:28). The Church is also God's flock, and kings, like David, can be its shepherds. If they neglect their duty and wolves harm the sheep, God will hold them accountable, just as Laban did with Jacob.

The Church is the pillar and foundation of truth, a field or garden where truth grows, and magistrates are the gardeners. They are obligated to nurture the good plants, remove weeds and stones that impede growth, and maintain a strong boundary to prevent corrupt influences, akin to the serpent in the Garden of Eden, from deceiving believers.

The Bible contains many examples and warnings for magistrates. In Revelation 2:20, God reproaches those who allow false teachers like Jezebel to mislead His servants. Every plant not planted by God should be uprooted (John 15:13), and it is the magistrates' duty to do this in God's vineyard.

In the Old Testament, the lives of magistrates are reflected as in a mirror, showing both their flaws and virtues. For instance, Jehoshaphat, in 2 Chronicles 17, commanded priests and Levites to teach the people the Law. He was devoted to the ways of the Lord and removed idolatrous high places and groves from Judah. Similarly, the actions of other kings, such as Solomon, Rehoboam, and Asa, are noted, highlighting their adherence to or deviation from God's laws and the consequences thereof. These examples show God's attention to even minor oversights and His disapproval of tolerance for worse matters.

In addition, the epistle of Jude urges *believers* to contend earnestly for the faith given once to the saints (Jude 3). This faith, given only once, must be guarded against corruption, as it will not be revealed again.

We should be grateful for our current situation under the rule of a gracious monarch, celebrating the public practice of religion and the ability to lead not only a peaceful but also an honest life. This blessing warrants heartfelt thankfulness to God and love for our rulers. We should obey them not just outwardly but inwardly, support them willingly, and pray for them sincerely.

As ministers of God, we boldly deliver God's impartial and inflexible rule, not shaped by human hands but molded by the Holy Spirit. This rule helps us identify our shortcomings and encourages us to promote truth and block the spread of heresies and errors, whether they be Popish, Arminian, or any other kind.

Walking closely with God brings peace, and any deviation from obedience is reflected in the blessings received. While wickedness may temporarily prosper, it will not endure, as Proverbs 12:3 suggests. Ultimately, righteousness will prevail, and the prosperity of the wicked will be short-lived. Those who are faithful to God may endure 68ardshipp but will eventually flourish. Good will befall those who fear God, and misfortune those who sin against Him. Uprightness and holiness lead to happiness, while sinfulness leads to misery.

# A Sensible Demonstration of the Deity

Isaiah 64:4, "For since the beginning of the world, men have not heard nor perceived by the ear, neither hath the eye seen another God, besides thee, which doth so to him that waiteth for him."

Isaiah 64:4 begins with the word "For," which has a reference to the previous verses. This connection also includes the third verse. In that verse, it is mentioned how God did unexpected and mighty things, causing even the mountains to flow down at His presence. Now, in Isaiah 64:4, the wording may differ in newer translations, but if you check the margins of your books, you'll likely find the same reading we currently use. This reading is in line with the original text and aligns better with the prophet's intent.

At first glance, the words in this verse may seem somewhat unclear, but in essence, it conveys this meaning: When the people of Israel faced formidable enemies more powerful than themselves, the prophet, speaking on behalf of the people, prayed to the Lord. Their prayer was for God to intervene dramatically, likened to breaking open the heavens and descending, causing even the mountains to flow down in His presence.

One might argue that their enemies were as formidable as mountains. However, the prophet emphasized that in God's presence, even mountains melt away, just as water boils when exposed to fire. The prayer was reinforced with the reasoning that God had done remarkable things in the past, both in punishing those who provoked Him and in blessing those who waited faithfully. Therefore, the plea was for God to act in the same way again—breaking open the heavens and descending.

If someone objected, suggesting that there might be other causes for the difficulties they faced, the prophet firmly denied it. He asserted that it was not within the power of creatures to bring about these changes. Only the Lord's descent, like fire melting wax or lead, could cause even the mightiest nations to crumble when He acted on their behalf.

If there were doubts about the existence of a God whose providence governed these events, the prophet provided an answer in the fourth verse: "For since the beginning of the world, men have not heard, nor perceived by the ear, neither hath the eye seen another God, besides thee, which doth such things for him that waiteth for him." In essence, he argued that while there were testimonies in the Scriptures, the words of the Prophets, and evidence of miracles affirming God's providence, one could simply look at the works of nature—things seen and heard—to recognize the existence of God. It was evident that God was responsible for the remarkable and unexpected events that occurred.

To summarize, three key points arise from these words:

1. It is clear, from what we see and hear every day, that God exists and performs extraordinary acts that we do not anticipate.

2. This God is the one and only God, and idols and false gods have no genuine existence.

3. He both punishes those who provoke Him with terrible deeds and blesses those who patiently await His intervention with great and wondrous acts.

These points find support in both Scripture and the natural world, confirming the existence of a God who actively governs all things.

Some creatures have distinctive characteristics that allow you to identify them. Among these characteristics, one of the most significant for rational creatures is the belief in God and the recognition that His providence governs all things, both in heaven and on earth.

Even though it might seem that no one doubts this, these proofs are valuable. They serve not only to counter the hidden objections of atheism, which we *all* occasionally harbor, but also to strengthen the fundamental principle that God exists. This principle is crucial in the foundation of all Christian faith and must bear the weight of the entire structure. Therefore, do not think that the proofs we will use to demonstrate this truth are unnecessary. Whenever the Scriptures speak, it is essential for us to listen attentively.

Firstly, if we contemplate the universe in general and examine the creation of heaven and earth, we can easily discern the eternal power and divinity of the Creator. Consider a person raised and brought up in a deep cave within the earth, where a dwelling and necessary provisions are provided. When this person, upon reaching maturity and understanding, is brought to the surface of the earth, they witness the magnificent beauty of the Sun, feel its warmth, experience the force of the winds, observe the swiftness of the clouds, the tides of the seas, and the changing of the seasons. They witness the celestial bodies moving across the heavens and the awe-inspiring darkness that follows the setting of the sun. Finally, they see the moon and stars illuminate the night for the benefit of humanity and animals. Would they not be filled with wonder at all these things that we often take for granted? There is a true saying: "Sapientis est rerum manifestarum causas quaerere," which means that a wise person seeks the causes of obvious things, while others overlook them and do not inquire into the reasons behind them.

In this quest for understanding, when this person realizes that humans are the highest of all creatures and yet are unable to create a roof like the heavens or a foundation like the earth, they must conclude that someone greater and more capable than humans is the Creator of all these things, which humans could not create on their own.

If it is argued that this Creator is not visible, even though the creation is visible, the answer is simple. Just as when you see a magnificent palace, you may not see the builder, but you still recognize that it could not have been constructed without a wise architect whose skill matched the grandeur of the work. Similarly, when you see a beautiful river flowing, even though you cannot see the spring from which it originates, you conclude that there must be a source somewhere that produces these streams. In the same way, when we observe the succession of creatures passing through generations, a wise person will say, "Surely there is a principle, a first cause, a source, from which they flow," even if it is not visible.

However, this is a general observation. If we explore the specific examination of creatures, it becomes even more evident through what we see and hear that there is a God whose providence governs *all* things. Let us consider the following examples:

First, we can observe the harmony that arises from the countless differences and contradictions among creatures. When we look at the structure of the world, we see one element opposing another: fire combating water, dryness opposing moisture, and moisture countering dryness, and so on. Yet, despite these contradictions, they come together in a harmonious way to build and maintain the entire universe. How could this be achieved without a wise Creator?

If you were to find an instrument with twenty discordant strings, all brought into perfect harmony, you would conclude that a skillful musician had tuned it. Similarly, when we examine the world and witness so many opposing elements ultimately harmonizing, must we not acknowledge the existence of a wise Agent who intends one thing and remits another, creating a useful fusion of all? This is the first observation we should make. How could so many contradictions coexist if they were not guided by someone greater than themselves?

Another aspect that demonstrates the existence of God, as seen and heard in creation, is the fitting and arrangement of one thing to another. For instance, if we entered the workshop of a skilled joiner or a meticulous smith and found everything perfectly fitted to each other—sheaths to knives, scabbards to swords—we would not attribute it to chance but to artistry. Likewise, when we explore the workshop of Nature and find that all the works of Nature are meticulously coordinated, must we not acknowledge a higher and wiser Creator who has orchestrated all of this?

Consider, for example, the creation of the *human eye*. God created the eye and provided it with the ability to perceive colors. But without the existence of light to reveal those colors, the eye's creation would serve no purpose. God also created colors, but without an intermediary transparent medium like air to transmit those colors to the eye, the purpose would still be unfulfilled. However, when we see all these components fitted perfectly together—eye, colors, light, and a medium for transmission—we recognize the result as a useful and perfect creation. The same principle applies to the rest of creation. The very things that we see with our eyes and hear with our ears make it evident that there is a God who has crafted all these things. If we examine the structure of the world and other specific details, we will find similar evidence.

Consider the plants that extend their roots into the earth to draw nourishment. They need no motion and are not given any motion. They possess a natural ability to spread their roots for added stability.

In contrast, consider the animals. They do not find nourishment where they are born, so they require motion. Consequently, they are *given* motion. Their movements vary based on their habitats—some crawl, some walk, some fly. Their different diets correspond to various adaptations, with some having teeth, others beaks, and some gums. Moreover, they exhibit distinct appetites, tastes, and smells according to their unique constitutions. All these creatures and their characteristics are perfectly matched to their environments and habits. If there were any disparities or incongruities, the entire system would be in vain.

Examining the creatures of the world and the intricacies of their design and interaction makes it evident that there is indeed a God whose providence governs all things, as seen and heard in the natural world.

If you were to take a watch into your hand and observe the intricately fitted wheels within it, you would acknowledge that this craftsmanship is not the result of chance but of *deliberate* design. Now, when you see a similar intricate design within the human body, where numerous bones, arteries, and sinews are all meticulously fitted together, should we not recognize a profound providence that has orchestrated all of this? This is the second point to consider.

The third observation arises from the actions of brute and irrational creatures such as the stork, the swallow, and the elephant. These creatures often perform actions that surpass their understanding and exceed their physical capabilities. For instance, they pursue goals they do not comprehend, follow rules they cannot grasp, employ means to achieve those goals, yet remain ignorant of the ultimate purpose. All of this suggests that they are guided by someone who knows both the destination they aim for and the path leading to it. Just as when a person navigates a complex route with many turns and eventually reaches the desired destination, they acknowledge that someone who knows the way guided them through those turns. Similarly, when we observe these creatures consistently perform actions without understanding them, it is evidence that there is an almighty power working within and through them. This leads to the saying of the Schoolmen, "Opus Naturae," which means that the work of Nature is not the work of Nature alone but *the work of the Author of Nature.* Therefore, when creatures exhibit wisdom and providence in their actions despite lacking these qualities in themselves, it indicates they are directed by a higher power. Just as you would recognize the guidance of an experienced hand in the elegant writing of a novice, you must acknowledge that these creatures, unaware of their goals and means, are directed by an all-knowing Power.

A fourth aspect by which the existence of the invisible things, namely the eternal power and Godhead, is made evident through the things that can be seen and heard, is the providential care provided for all creatures. Imagine entering a well-organized society or household where everything is arranged orderly, with food provided for all members in due time and season. In such a case, you would not doubt the presence of a governing authority responsible for maintaining this order.

Should we not then acknowledge the same when we see it on a grand scale in the vast household of the world, where countless millions of humans and animals are daily fed, clothed, and ordered? Consider a small family—if even a minor lapse in providence occurs, the entire family quickly feels the effects. How, then, do we think that the vast family of the world could be sustained without a special providence overseeing it? For instance, in feeding so many creatures, if humans were tasked with providing their sustenance, where would they begin? God has commanded the earth to produce grass as sustenance, just as He has commanded the skins of animals to yield hair, feathers, and wool for suitable clothing. Moreover, His providence extends to protecting and defending creatures from each other's harm. Some creatures possess hooves, horns, and tusks for defense, while others with lesser natural protection have the ability to flee. Those without either of these advantages find refuge in holes and dens. Notably, weaker creatures gather in herds for safety, while the stronger ones often go solo; for if they banded together, no human or beast could withstand them. This principle is stated in Job 37 and Psalm 104. If the Queen of Sheba, upon witnessing the wisdom and provision in Solomon's court, was astonished (1 Kings 10), how much more should we admire and acknowledge the great providence of God when we consider this vast household of the world where countless beings rise and rest, all in need of daily sustenance? We should recognize that it is God who "openeth his hand and giveth them their meat in due season." This forms the fourth observation.

The fifth observation arises from the interconnectedness and interdependence among creatures. Humans rely on animals for food, animals depend on plants for nourishment, and plants require the influence of the heavens to grow. This subordination is expressed in Hosea 2:21: "I will hear the heavens, and the heavens shall hear the earth, and the earth shall hear the corn." This leads us to a logical conclusion: either this intricate order and connection resulted from mere chance or from providence. It cannot be attributed to chance, just as one cannot claim that a jumble of letters thrown together by chance can create a coherent history or poem. Therefore, when we observe this order, connection, and interdependence among creatures, it is clear that it was not by chance but by providence. Just as a well-composed piece of writing with sentences and words interconnected and dependent upon each other cannot exist without the art of wit and reason in its author, the same applies to the interdependence of creatures.

The final observation is drawn from the wisdom of the Creator, which is clearly evident in all of His works, just as the skill of an artist is evident in everything they create. When we behold a finely crafted statue of a man, we readily acknowledge that it was skillfully made by the person who created it. Shouldn't we then acknowledge the same divine wisdom in the Maker of man himself? Similarly, when we encounter a glass eye, an ivory tooth, or a wooden leg, we attribute their creation to a skillful artisan. Shouldn't we, therefore, recognize a special providence and wisdom in the creation of human body parts? In fact, things created by nature are often superior to those created by human artistry, for art merely imitates nature, and that which is imitated is superior to the imitation. Hence, we attribute skill and wisdom to the works of art, but should we not attribute the same, if not more, to the works of nature, which far surpass them?

Consider a sundial that accurately marks the hours of the day; we acknowledge that it was created by the skill of a human being. When we observe the same precision in the heavens, governing times and seasons, shouldn't we recognize the wisdom of the One who created and guides the heavens? It is said that Archimedes crafted a sphere in which the movements of the heavens, the course of the sun, and the ebb and flow of the sea were accurately described and maintained in the order of their natural movements. When a person sees this, they readily conclude that it was not the result of chance but the skill of an *exceptional* artist. If that is the case, then surely the actual phenomena that the sphere imitates can only be the result of the wondrous power and wisdom of the One who accomplishes it. I will not delve further into this but proceed to make some practical applications.

First and foremost, in addition to the testimony of Scripture, there are numerous proofs evident from what our eyes see and our ears hear that affirm the existence of God, by whose *providence* all things come to pass. This should strengthen our faith in the fundamental and primary principle *that God exists*. While even a small light can reveal an object, the addition of more arguments should illuminate that object more clearly and distinctly. Therefore, though we believe by faith that God exists, the accumulation of these arguments should fortify our belief and confirm this conclusion, leading us to a more steadfast assent. My beloved, although it may go unnoticed, it is a certainty that much of the moral imperfection and waywardness in human lives results from a wavering faith in these foundational principles. People do not completely disregard religion, nor do they fully commit their hearts to God in all matters. The reason for this is that these foundational principles are only *partially* believed. In other words, people may think in their hearts that perhaps there is an Almighty God who created heaven and earth, or perhaps not. As a result, they may attend to some religious duties, but their devotion is not wholehearted. If they believed fully, they would serve God with complete and perfect hearts.

Is this the only application to be made from this? Is this the sole purpose the Prophet intends to convey in this passage? No, his primary aim is to show us that if such a God exists, then it is He who orchestrates the extraordinary events that befall us—they do not occur by mere chance. Therefore, we present the point that through what our eyes see and our ears hear, it becomes evident that there is a God who performs both terrible and merciful deeds, both good and evil occurrences that happen to us. Consequently, we should live by faith, not by mere sensory perception, which means that we should fear God and seek Him while there is still time, lest we experience unexpected and dreadful events. For even though we believe that such a God exists, if we do not live accordingly, we forget the Lord and live as if He does not exist.

When adversity strikes, every person reacts with alarm, just as a beast struggles to escape when it falls into a pit or bog. Yet the highest form of faith and wisdom lies in anticipating and averting future calamities. Saul sought the Lord when he was in dire straits, but the Lord did not answer him through prophets or Urim and Thummim. Joab, in his extremity and with no other refuge, sought refuge at the horns of the altar, just as people resort to prayer in times of sickness, danger, and extremity. But then it was too late. Esau sought the blessing with tears, but only when it was beyond help and recovery. Why did they not act sooner, while there was still time? This delay is undoubtedly rooted in a hidden atheism and unbelief that afflicts us all to some degree. It prevents us from being moved by early warnings until we feel the full force of the impending evil. Therefore, it is said here that terrible things happen to us that we did not anticipate.

Death is a terrifying prospect, yet because we perceive it as distant, we often neglect to contemplate the brevity of life while there is still time to secure our calling and election, so that our souls do not depend on uncertainties. Hell is a *dreadful* thought—considering the immortality of the soul and the existence of an eternal dwelling place—but how many truly contemplate it in time and *take it to heart*? External calamities that befall a church, a state, or an individual are fearful, yet how often do we anticipate and take measures to prevent them? This is the nature of humanity throughout the ages. We think we will act "just in time," but we keep *delaying*. Thus, we are drawn further and further away from taking actions that could have averted the impending evils. And so, terrible things happen to us, things we did not foresee.

The underlying cause of this procrastination is partly due to our tendency to live by sensory perception rather than by faith. We all, to varying degrees, think that our present circumstances will continue unchanged, whether they are afflictions or prosperity. If we are in distress, we assume it will last forever, and if we are prosperous, we often presume that "tomorrow shall be as today, and much more abundant." This is a natural inclination. Furthermore, it is because we witness dangers come and go, dissipate and pass away, without experiencing their full impact that we become complacent. We behave like the fool who, seeing the river gradually receding, waits on the shore, hoping it will soon be completely dry so he can cross without difficulty. We forget that there is a continuous flow of water, which will persist. Similarly, we overlook the fact that God possesses an arsenal of sorrows; even if He afflicts us seven times, He can add seven times more. However, if we remain obstinate, He can add seven times more. Until eventually, His wrath overflows its banks, sweeping everything before it. This concept is expressed in the prophecy of Nahum.

Furthermore, this procrastination occurs because God is often unseen and forgotten in the world.

The very creatures that should serve as a clear mirror through which we might perceive God instead often become thick clouds obscuring Him from our view. We gaze at the wall of creation but fail to see the Creator standing behind it, the One who changes times and seasons as He governs the weather. Our understanding of God becomes as uncertain as predicting rain, snow, or wind. We engage in forecasting future events, just as we calculate days and years, forgetting that God, the One who disposes of these, is the ultimate authority.

And so, let us be encouraged to consider it our greatest wisdom to *anticipate* the most significant danger that may come while it is still distant. Just as fire can be ignited far away from the target of its intended explosion in a train of gunpowder, the Romans wisely observed that when Hannibal was besieging Siguntium, a city allied with them, they considered every blow struck against it as if he were attacking the walls of the Capitol in Rome itself, even though Siguntium was a considerable distance away. They took equal care to prevent the danger, as if it had already reached their doorstep. Similarly, when the enemy assails the distant churches, he is effectively striking at the very foundation of this Church and Commonwealth.

A fundamental principle to understand is that when the day of calamity arrives, it is a time for spending, not gathering. Preparations must be made *beforehand*. It is futile to seek oil when it is needed or to go out and buy it when the Bridegroom arrives. This is why the foolish virgins are called so because *folly is imprudent*; it remains in the valley and *does not perceive* the impending danger. Wisdom, on the other hand, stands upon a hill, discerning distant threats before they draw near. It is undeniable (allow me to speak, for we are the watchmen on the tower and should see more than those below; we must issue warnings to save our own souls, lest your blood be required of us) that evil intentions are directed toward us and will come upon us unless something is done to prevent them. God has made a covenant with us, and a breach of that covenant leads to quarrels. God's quarrel will not go unanswered, for He declares to the Israelites in Leviticus 26:25 that He will send a sword upon them to avenge *the quarrel of His covenant*.

Even if we are skeptical of His word, can we deny His actions? Have we not seen the entire body of those who profess the truth besieged throughout Christendom? Are not our allies weakened? Have not many branches of the Church already been severed, with more at risk? Have not our endeavors been repeatedly frustrated and withered away? Have things not been declining for a long time and are now approaching a conclusion? And do we attribute such events solely to accidents and mishaps, or do we recognize the ultimate cause? Are these not warning signs before the fall of the house? Are they not the gray hairs spoken of by the prophet Hosea, indicative of old age and impending death?

Surely, God has begun a work among us, and He will not abandon it halfway. As it is said in 1 Samuel 3:12, "When I begin, I will make an end." Samuel had pronounced fearful judgments against the house of Eli, and although they lived in peace for a while and the judgments were not immediately executed, God assured them that when He began, He would also complete His work. For our own sake and for the sake of the churches, let us seriously consider this. There is undoubtedly a reason for God's displeasure, and until it is rectified, the Lord will not return to us and grant us prosperity in our endeavors.

When Joshua saw the people falling before their enemies, he inquired about the cause, and unless that cause had been addressed, the success of bringing the children of Israel to the land of Canaan would have been in jeopardy, despite God's promise. God's promises, like His warnings, come with conditions. In 2 Samuel 21:1, during a famine in David's time, he recognized the natural cause as drought but sought the supernatural cause. Wise individuals inquire into supernatural causes, while fools only focus on immediate circumstances. Therefore, in times of calamity, we should search for the underlying cause, whether affecting the Church in general or individuals in particular.

There are seasons when God troubles the churches, and usually, when He does so for one, He does it for all. There is a connection, for when any affliction befalls a nation, church, or individual, it is because God is displeased, and He is never angered without cause, unlike the passing anger of humans. Therefore, we should seek to remove the cause of His anger and plead with the Lord before His judgment is executed. Just as destruction can be averted, it can also come in unexpected ways, and God's judgments find paths we do not foresee. Thus, it is vital for us to recognize the season in which we live.

Two instances highlight the importance of discerning seasons. When Jerusalem faced captivity, the Lord spent over twenty years giving warnings through His prophets and bringing Nebuchadnezzar close before executing judgment. The people's failure was their inability to discern the season of impending judgment. Similarly, when the famine came during David's reign, its supernatural cause was traced back to Saul's broken oath with the Gibeonites, many years earlier. In both cases, discerning the season and addressing the cause could have prevented the calamity.

In conclusion, it is crucial to recognize the signs of the times and discern the seasons in which we live. God's judgments and blessings are contingent upon our response to His warnings and our willingness to address the underlying causes of His displeasure. Wisdom dictates that we fear and depart from evil, seek the Lord in times of trouble, and remove the things that provoke His anger. Just as the stork and cranes discern their seasons, so should we discern the seasons of God's judgments and blessings, for His actions are purposeful and just. May we heed these warnings and act accordingly, for there is a time for preparation and a time for execution, and we must discern the difference.

# Exact Walking

Eph. 5:15, "Take heed that you walk therefore circumspectly (or *exactly*) not as fools, but as wise."

In the eighth verse of this chapter, the Apostle lays down this conclusion, "You were once darkness, but now you are light in the Lord, walk therefore as children of the light;" this he emphasizes with some arguments, and draws some consequences from it, among which this is one: "Take heed, therefore, that you walk *exactly*, not as fools, but as wise." It's as if he is saying, "Now that the darkness is gone, now that you are set upon a hill, now that you are in the broad light that all can see, look after yourselves. Ensure that you walk in an exact and wise manner, not foolishly." So, in these words:

First, there is a command or an exhortation placed upon them, "Walk circumspectly," or "exactly."

Secondly, this command is supported by a reason, "Not as fools, but as wise," implying that it is wise to do so, and folly to act otherwise.

Thirdly, a means to accomplish this is given, "Take heed," or "Consider." This means it's not an easy task and requires careful attention. A person may perform an action without much thought, but if they want to do it exactly, they must be *cautious*.

I will explain the words in detail as I address them. However, I must explain, it is the most beneficial course of action for ourselves, surpassing all other actions, to walk exactly before Christ. Consider all the actions that proceed straightforwardly; they improve something external to a person, but they do not improve the heart of the individual. When it comes to teaching others, the perfection of the scholar lies in it. Other actions related to wealth, honor, learning, or anything of that nature enhance the object they are focused on. However, this particular action, in which the heart turns inward upon itself, this reflective action, is what perfects a person's soul. It makes a person a better individual and builds them up in grace and truth. When a person introspects and turns inward, they mend the flaws in their heart. If there is anything amiss there, they rectify it. Therefore, it is an action that we should readily accept, and we should heed the Apostle's exhortation. To conclude this point, let us be encouraged to reflect on our actions. The failure to do so is the cause of numerous errors in our lives, wasted hours, vain speeches, and gross sins committed—all due to a lack of consideration. If the person who swears would carefully consider what it means when the Lord says, "I will not hold him guiltless that taketh my Name in vain," they would not be so quick to swear. If the adulterer would consider what God says, "Whoremongers and adulterers God will judge," they would not so *easily* continue in that sin. You can apply this to other specific situations, so consideration is necessary in matters related to salvation. It is not the same in other matters; in other matters, the idea quickly passes from the mind to the rest of the faculties. As soon as the thought arises, it is immediately executed. However, in matters related to *godliness*, there may be a spark, and it will go out again in the heart, just as green wood extinguishes a fire. In such cases, *effort* must be exerted due to the stubbornness of the faculties of the mind in obeying the light of Christ dictated to the conscience. Therefore, in this case, we must treat it as we do with stubborn servants; they must be instructed to do something again; they must be compelled to do it. If the lower faculties were as willing to obey the mind in spiritual matters as they are in other matters, it would be a different situation. In other matters, for the most part, you will find that as soon as the mind resolves to do something, the faculties are immediately ready to practice and execute it. If it concerns pleasure, profit, or business, once a person decides to do it, they encounter no resistance. However, if it concerns a holy life, even though a person is determined and fully intends to do it, they encounter *numerous* obstacles in the lower faculties. These obstacles are like stubborn servants that require coercion and imperative commands. Therefore, *consideration* is necessary for us. If we neglect it, leading a holy life becomes impossible because we encounter obstacles in that regard. Every good action requires this consideration, and we should do it all the more because it is what perfects us the most. We study many things—books, people, and ourselves—and this is accomplished through the act of consideration. Among all studies, studying one's own heart when one dwells within is the best. It was the advice of the wise moralist to encourage people to dwell within themselves, to look inward. A person should be like a diligent housewife in their own house, tidying up the rooms of their heart, sweeping every morning, and putting things in order that were disarrayed the previous day. This is so that they may be fit to receive Jesus Christ the Lord of glory. Therefore, we should strive to keep ourselves in order, to keep ourselves clean and pure in both soul and body through this continual act of consideration. This way, we may become suitable temples for the Holy Ghost to dwell in and abide in. Hence, we should engage in this practice.

First, in general, consider your condition, contemplate why you came into the world. Sit down and reflect upon the fact that you have an immortal soul that will exist in another place for eternity. Your life is uncertain, and you do not know when your soul will be taken from you. If a person would consider these things, if they would sit down and ponder their ultimate fate, consider the certainty of God's threats, contemplate the uncertainty of life, and reflect on the terror of God's wrath, they would not continue in a course of sin. This is what the people failed to do, as Moses pointed out in Deuteronomy 29:4. He said that the people had seen what the Lord did to Pharaoh and all his servants, they had witnessed the temptations and great works He performed, but they did not have hearts to perceive, and they did not have eyes to see. In other words, they did not have hearts to consider. Even though these were strong reasons to fear God, it availed them nothing because they did not have hearts to consider. Similarly, when Christ performed the miracle of walking on water in Mark 6:52, the disciples did not consider the miracle of the loaves, and that's why they were afraid. The miracles should have strengthened their faith, but they did not profit from them because they did not consider. In 2 Timothy 2:6, Paul exhorts Timothy to consider what he says, and he prays to God for understanding in *all* things. We are not able to do this on our own, so we should beseech God to open our eyes and enable us to consider. Until He sets us to work, we cannot do it effectively.

Some might say, "Is it necessary for a person to consider every action they take?" I say that it is not necessary for every action to be carefully considered. Just as in a journey, it's not required for a person to think about *every* step; the initial intention of the journey will take them a long way. Similarly, if you set your heart on the right path, that intention will guide you through many actions without the need to consider every detail. However, because our hearts are prone to stray, like young horses unaccustomed to the road, they tend to veer off course unless the reins are held continuously. Therefore, this consideration must be repeated in the heart to keep it on track, or it is apt to deviate. This practice must be learned in matters related to *godliness* because in other matters, people are already inclined to do it. Young men consider how to satisfy their flesh and desires, how to attain pleasures. Older individuals consider how to increase their wealth and maintain connections. There is already too much consideration given to external advantages. What we truly need is to consider how we can lead a *circumspect and holy life* before Jesus Christ in all things. Neglecting this and focusing on other matters is no different than madness. If a person seriously considers what they are and their condition, they would regard it as madness to pursue other things as they do. Just as we consider people mad when they gather straw, decorate their clothes with flowers, or scribble on walls because we view these actions as unfit for a person. Similarly, when Christians are occupied with trivial matters, pleasures, and honors (for they are no better), and they pursue these with all their effort, it is as unfitting for a Christian as those actions I mentioned are below a person. It is truly spiritual madness, just as the other is natural insanity. Therefore, consider this and come to your senses. I am not being too harsh in calling it madness; the Scripture refers to it in this way. In Luke 15, the Prodigal Son is said to have "come to himself," meaning he had already done so for other matters, but not for matters of self-preservation, grace and salvation. So, one can truthfully say that the world is full of madmen in this sense because they fall short of what is expected of a Christian, of what is expected of a person in relation to God and eternity, just as the mentioned actions are below other people. You will find that they are occupied in a similar manner. Look at people's activities, and if we could see what they are truly busy with, their thoughts and lives, we would see them acting like madmen. They are like a person making a garland for themselves, composed of the vanity they are most enamored with. Therefore, consider what you do, "Walk *circumspectly*, not as fools, but as wise" (Ephesians 5:15). Walk exactly.

Now, let's move on to the main point: "Walk exactly." Therefore, consider that you should "walk exactly." We will deliver this doctrine as it is stated: It is required of a Christian that he walk with God exactly in all things. Before I consider this point, let me explain what this "walking" means and what it means to "walk exactly."

In short, "walking" refers to the course and path of a person's life. So, to "walk holily" means to adhere closely to the rules in all aspects and situations of life. It means maintaining the same standard no matter the circumstances, whether alone or in company, in times of leisure or business, among enemies or friends. It means consistently living by the same principles, whether the outcome benefits or harms you, whether you are in a pleasant situation or not. A person should not compromise or seek inventions that will eventually crumble like untempered mortar. Instead, their conscience should guide them, and they should willingly obey it. When a person behaves this way consistently in their daily life, it is "walking exactly."

But what about the term "exact"? The Greek word for "exact" comes from two words that mean *going to the extremity of a thing*. So, "walking exactly" means keeping God's commandments to the *utmost*, not just doing the main duties but paying attention to *every* detail. The Apostle's purpose here is to commend what is often disapproved of in the world, namely, exactness or preciseness. This word may be translated as preciseness, and there is no word in Greek that fits better. We should recognize that preciseness is the true excellence of a Christian. Just as the best mirror reveals the smallest spots, the brightest light exposes the tiniest specks, and the finest flesh feels the slightest pricks, the conscience that is sensitive to the least sin or failing is the pinnacle of Christianity. It should be far from being disdained by us.

To "walk exactly" is required of everyone, and this exactness involves three conditions:

First, consider the whole rule. To do a business exactly, you must not look at just a part of it; you need to regard all the commandments and precepts found in the book of God.

Secondly, one must go to the *utmost* extent in keeping every commandment. Our Savior teaches this in Matthew 5. It's not enough for a person not to commit murder; they must also refrain from becoming angry with their brother unjustly. This shows the extremity of the command. Not only should one take care of the main commandments but also observe the least of them. Jesus says that a person should not swear great oaths or break their oaths but let their yes be yes and their no be no (Matthew 5). Similarly, for the commandment "Thou shalt not commit adultery," if a person even entertains lustful and adulterous thoughts in their heart, they are not walking exactly. They must realize that failing in any part of the commandments means they shall not enter into Heaven. Therefore, they must consider the entire rule and every particular command.

Lastly, this exactness must be maintained at all times. Psalm 106, verse 3, says, "Blessed is he that doth justice and loves righteousness at all times." Without consistency, a person cannot be exact. If someone only practices exactness occasionally or sporadically, if they walk exactly one day and then stray from it another, they cannot be considered as walking exactly. They are inconsistent and walk with God intermittently, just as one who only regards half of the rule or walks only part of the way. If either of these is the case—walking partially or intermittently—one cannot be exact.

Now, let's discuss why this exactness is necessary. It is required in three respects:

Firstly, in regard to a person's character, they must be adorned with all the graces of the Spirit. There should be no deficiency in this regard. In 2 Peter 1, we see that graces are listed together. "And beside this, giving all diligence, add to your faith virtue; and to virtue knowledge; and to knowledge temperance; and to temperance patience; and to patience godliness; and to godliness brotherly kindness; and to brotherly kindness charity. For if these things be in you, and abound, they make you that ye shall neither be barren nor unfruitful in the knowledge of our Lord Jesus Christ," (2 Peter 1:5-8). A Christian should not be adorned with only *some* of the graces but should possess all of them. They must be exact and have the entire clothing, the complete image of God. If any of these graces are lacking, it will result in a significant defect. For example, if a person has faith but lacks virtue, meaning their faith does not manifest in works, their faith is *useless*. If someone is zealous and eager for work but lacks knowledge to guide and direct them, they will *err* greatly. Therefore, they must join knowledge with virtue. If someone has knowledge to know what to do but does not put the practice of other graces into action, such as being temperate, their conduct will be *incongruous*. Even if someone has other virtues but lacks one, such as patience, they fall short of what God expects. In this way, a Christian should be adorned with every grace because God requires such beauty. In Song of Solomon 4:7, Christ tells his Church, "Thou art all fair, my love; there is no spot in thee," indicating that the Church is adorned with all the graces of the Spirit, without any lacking. A generality of graces is required for the beauty of a man in Christ. Christ is said to work "grace for grace," meaning for every grace in himself, he has instilled another in us. Every Christian possesses these graces to some extent, though not in the same degree as Christ. Nevertheless, they must be exact in all respects concerning their character.

Secondly, exactness is required regarding a person's actions. All the actions a holy person performs must be exact. According to the Schoolmen, an action cannot be considered good unless every aspect of it is good. If any part or circumstance of an action is lacking, the action is evil. To pray without fervency, to show mercy without cheerfulness, to observe the Sabbath without delight—any deficiency in these circumstances makes an action evil. Therefore, exactness is necessary concerning a person's actions.

Thirdly, exactness is required concerning others. In James 1, it is stated, "Pure religion and undefiled before God and the Father is this, To visit the fatherless and widows in their affliction, and to keep himself unspotted from the world." To remain unspotted by the world, one must be exact in all things. Even though we should not eagerly seek the world's applause, every Christian should strive to be blameless in their conduct. They should be unblemished from top to toe, so to speak, as any slight deviation from exactness can lead to the world smearing their reputation. While seeking the world's praise is not the goal, Christians should endeavor to be blameless in all their interactions. They should aim to be like Zacharias and Elizabeth, who walked in all the commandments without reproof. In this regard, a Christian must walk exactly in relation to their own character, their actions, and others.

Now, a question or objection arises concerning this point I have presented. When I say that it is *required* of Christians, the question is whether it is *absolutely* necessary, whether they cannot maintain a good relationship with God, whether they cannot have assurance of their own salvation unless they walk exactly. Is such strictness imposed on them that they have no other option but to maintain this level of exactness in their conduct?

In response to this, I would say that this commandment, like any other in *the Book of God*, should be observed with an Evangelical spirit, even if we cannot keep it strictly under the Law. This means we *must make every effort* within our power to fulfill it. We should strive with all our might, purpose to do it, and put forth efforts consistent with our intentions. Every person is obliged to walk in an *exact* manner, which means not allowing oneself to engage in any known sin. There may be instances of failing due to passion or being carried away by unawareness, but when it comes to a known sin that one allows in their life, it breaches the Evangelical observance of this Commandment, which requires one to walk *exactly*. This necessity applies to everyone – to abstain from any known sin in their conduct. Walking exactly is revealed through the following reasons.

First, if there is even a single aspect in your behavior, be it major or minor, that becomes a known sin, and you know that such a thing is a duty or a sin, if you do not walk exactly in that matter, it creates a separation between you and God. Just as in the case of two friends who have a minor difference that, if not resolved, creates a complete division between them, the same applies here. Even if it concerns a less significant matter, such as the least sin or the neglect of the least duty, when you know that God requires it, not adhering to it creates a breach. It *separates you from God*, as it would with a rebel against a prince's command. Therefore, any resistance to God in your conduct, if you are not exact in all things, leads to a state of separation from God.

Second, unless a person walks exactly with God in all things, it is evident that what they do, they do for themselves and not for the Lord, and if it is not done for the Lord, it is *not accepted* by God. When a person performs obedience for the Lord and His commandments to please Him, why would they set limits for themselves? God requires that we do His will on earth *as it is done in Heaven*. His command is for us to go to the utmost in every commandment. When we restrict ourselves in holiness, when we think, "I will do only enough to reach Heaven, I will strive for a certain level of exactness in my conduct just to stay in a state of grace and avoid hell," it is purely self-centered. Such an attitude is self-love. When a person focuses only on their own salvation and how to escape hell, they cannot be considered right. When they impose limits on themselves and refrain from going to the utmost, it signifies that their heart *is not upright*. Therefore, there is a necessity for everyone to *walk exactly* with God in all things.

Third, consider any specific aspect of a person's behavior in which they indulge themselves. If they are overcome by it, it means they are not in Christ. Those in Christ overcome the world, the flesh, and the devil. In Galatians 5, the Apostle says, "Whosoever is in Christ crucifieth the flesh and the affections." They also overcome the devil, just as the stronger man casts out the strong man. However, if a particular sin tempts a person, and they yield to it, they are overcome. None of those in Christ are overcome by the world, the flesh, or the devil. In other words, if any particular sin leads a person to yield and give up the fight, they are said to be *overcome*. While those who continue to fight against sin are in a different situation, *giving in* signifies being overcome.

Fourth, if there is any specific sin in a person's behavior that they allow, it hinders the effectiveness of all means and renders them unprofitable. They will be unable to pray, listen, or perform any duty as they should. Just as a medicine is ineffective as long as the arrowhead remains in the wound, it must be removed first for the cure to take effect. Similarly, if even one sin or failing in exactness exists in a person's conduct, all the means of grace become futile. Hence, there is a necessity for every person, if they want to be a Christian and consider themselves among the children of light, to walk exactly. Without further ado, I'll proceed to make some brief application of this, as I aim to address the other aspect, "Not as fools, but as wise."

The practical use we should make of this is to engage in the work, to actually do what is required, and to strive to walk with great *precision*. It's beneficial to focus on specific aspects of our lives. Take, for example, the observance of the Lord's Day. I'd like to pose a question: Is this day not meant to be holy? Does it not differ from ordinary days? If it is indeed holy, should it not be observed as such, with exactness and devotion to God? The same applies to prayer. When you call upon the name of God, He does not desire a *superficial* performance of the duty. He values the *quality* rather than the quantity of your prayers. Therefore, make sure to pray with *exactness*. This principle extends to receiving the sacrament and all other duties. I encourage you to think about the specifics.

Regarding your daily work and responsibilities, be diligent in them. Serve God and others with enthusiasm and dedication. When it comes to sports and recreation, be precise in your choices. Avoid engaging in unlawful activities, and even in lawful ones, do not indulge excessively. Approach them with moderation and proper intentions. In all your dealings with people, in every situation and circumstance in your life, ensure that you *walk with precision*. Your obedience should be comprehensive. If it isn't, it may indicate that your heart has not truly changed. A person is not truly born again until they are willing to perform every duty and avoid every sin they are aware of. If your heart is right, you will have an aversion to anything that is considered sinful. What is the value of religion if we only practice easy and convenient duties for which we have no inclination? True power in religion lies in subduing every desire and inclination, and obeying God even in the face of great difficulties, especially during times of temptation and trials. This is necessary for us. Without this commitment to exactness, we end up serving our own desires rather than God. As James 2 states, "For he that said, Do not commit adultery, said also, Do not kill." Therefore, if you fail in any particular aspect or allow yourself to persist in any known sin, you should consider that God has also commanded you in that area. Why do you not obey in all things? Just as a small leak can sink a ship and one disease can take a life, one sin or one failure in exactness in your conduct is enough to destroy you and place you in an unfavorable condition before God. Therefore, strive to walk with precision and avoid detours. Even though these may be hidden from human eyes, God sees everything that occurs in secret.

It is a common practice for people to follow the crowd, outwardly conforming to societal norms, attending church, avoiding gross sins, living civilly, and acting justly in their everyday lives. However, they maintain a hidden course of their own, often yielding to their own desires and inclinations. We must labor to be precise and cautious, always aware that God observes us. The saints in the past have demonstrated that this is possible. It is not an unattainable goal. Look at Moses, who left nothing behind when God commanded him to leave Egypt. He did it with *precision*. Consider Paul, who maintained a clear conscience in all things. Look at Samuel, who invited the people to examine his actions, asking if he had wronged anyone or taken their possessions.

On the other hand, those who failed in this exactness and allowed themselves to indulge in specific sins illustrate that it is not a minor matter. Saul, for instance, walked with God but was rejected because he did not walk with *exactness*. He offered a sacrifice prematurely, which might seem insignificant, but because he spared Agag, God rejected him. Nadab and Abihu offered a sacrifice that may seem to involve minor details, such as the choice of fire, but they were consumed because they did not walk with exactness. The prophet who did not adhere closely to God's word was slain by a lion upon his return. Balaam, despite outward appearances, was rejected by God because he was not exact, and God saw the falseness of his heart. Therefore, be cautious and strive to walk with *precision*.

This is not foolishness but wisdom. It is wise to do *what God has appointed* and to follow the rule of wisdom, which commands us to walk with *precision*. It is wise to be guided by God, the wisest of all. Walking with exactness aligns with the properties of wisdom. Wisdom involves considering the ultimate and universal purpose of one's life and aligning all actions accordingly. A person who does not have a clear purpose and direction in their life, who behaves aimlessly or randomly, is displaying foolishness.

In addition to this, if a person lacks a purpose in life or has only a specific purpose, they cannot be considered truly wise. They may be skilled in a particular field, such as piloting, statesmanship, trade, or warfare, with specific objectives. However, one cannot be called wise unless they have a clear understanding of the overall direction and purpose of their life. The truly wise person, the one who walks perfectly with God, is wise because they correctly perceive the general framework and trajectory of their life. The root of many of our errors, as someone has stated, lies in our tendency to focus only on certain aspects of our lives, neglecting the whole. We fail to keep our eyes on the overarching purpose of our existence, leading us to act imprudently. Therefore, true wisdom is found in framing the entirety of one's life correctly, ensuring that their ultimate aim is righteous. This is why the Scripture equates wisdom with godliness and folly with wickedness, using the best and worst descriptors imaginable. Consequently, the wisest person, regardless of other accomplishments, is the one who walks with exactness with God.

Another aspect of wisdom is not merely knowing but also *implementing* that knowledge. This is what distinguishes prudence from other skills. In other disciplines, the person who possesses the knowledge of what is best is considered the most skilled. However, in matters of prudence, the one who knows what to do but fails to act is the most foolish of all. Therefore, wisdom is closely tied to action. A truly wise person is not only aware of what needs to be done but earnestly puts that knowledge into practice. It is not enough to judge individuals based on their knowledge or potential but rather by their actions, as the Apostle Paul declares, "God shall judge men according to their works."

Furthermore, wisdom entails considering not only one part of a situation but examining it from all angles. Error often arises when individuals fixate on one aspect that appeals to them without considering the potential drawbacks. This is where wisdom is crucial, and walking perfectly with God is the epitome of wisdom. For instance, when someone strays from the path of God and seeks personal gain or reputation, or when they indulge in sinful desires to satisfy temporary pleasures they believe will benefit them, it is because they lack wisdom. They focus solely on one part of the equation. If they were to consider the whole picture, if they were to connect the cause and effect, they would realize that their chosen path leads to misery, while abstaining from sin would bring happiness. But because they concentrate on one aspect and not the entirety, many do not walk with exactness.

Another aspect of wisdom involves looking beyond surface appearances and exploring the essence of things. Fools judge by outward appearances, while wise individuals discern the inner qualities. They see the life within the tree, not just the bark. When a person only sees the outward presentation, they are susceptible to snares, like being deceived by the bait while failing to notice the hidden hook. The most valuable things in the world often have humble exteriors, while lesser things are adorned with gilded surfaces. Lacking wisdom, many are drawn to the superficial glitter while ignoring the true value within. As the Apostle says, "We are as men of sorrow, though indeed we rejoice as men having nothing, though we possess all things." This means that outward appearances can be deceiving, and wisdom lies in discerning the reality beneath the surface. Those who walk with exactness possess this wisdom. For example, when Moses had to choose between suffering with the people of God, an outwardly difficult path, and enjoying the pleasures of sin and the treasures of Egypt, which had an attractive exterior, his wisdom enabled him to see the true nature of both choices. Those who *walk perfectly* with God see beyond appearances. I would have provided some exhortation, but our time is now over. This should suffice for today.

# Samuel's Support for Sorrowful Sinners

"And Samuel said unto the people, Fear not: ye have done all this wickedness: yet turn not aside from following the LORD, but serve the LORD with all your heart; And turn ye not aside: for then should ye go after vain things, which cannot profit nor deliver; for they are vain. For the LORD will not forsake his people for his great name's sake: because it hath pleased the LORD to make you his people." (1 Sam. 12:20-22).

The occasion for these words was as follows: In the earlier part of the chapter, Samuel had pointed out the great sin of the people in desiring a king, stating that they had *rejected* the Lord as their king. In response, God revealed His displeasure through a miraculous sign from heaven, which greatly alarmed the people. They feared and asked Samuel to pray for them. In these verses, Samuel addresses their fear and seeks to comfort them. He acknowledges their sin but assures them that God will continue to be merciful. He urges them not to turn away from following the Lord, warning against pursuing empty and unprofitable things. Samuel emphasizes that God will not forsake His people because of His great name's sake and His choice to make them His own.

The central lesson derived from these words is that human nature tends to have excessive and uncontrolled emotions, including fear, love, and grief.

Now, the fact that it was like this with them becomes evident from Samuel's speech. You can recognize the ailment by the remedy prescribed. Their hearts were greatly shaken and almost swayed away from the Lord. Therefore, he advises them not to be *excessively* afraid. This illustrates that we are prone to fear immoderately. Undoubtedly, they had prophets among them who had warned them of this sin all the time they were pursuing it. During that period, they had no fear. But when thunder came, they began to fear excessively, and Samuel had a challenging task to calm them down.

Inordinate affections occur when we fail to love, fear, or grieve *as we should*. This inordinacy exists either in deficiency, where we do not feel love, fear, or grief when appropriate, or in excess when we become overly attached to something. This excess can result from misdirecting our affections towards the wrong objects or exaggerating their intensity. This is where the error in our affections lies. Let's examine our own disposition through the disposition of these people: When we are in good health, we do not fear sin, but, as the Prophet puts it, we rush into sin as a horse rushes into battle. A horse cannot distinguish its enemies, and it charges ahead to its own destruction. Similarly, Solomon states that a fool proceeds and faces punishment, and a fool rages and is reckless. In other words, a fool is passionate in his affections towards sin and yet remains fearless. We can see this in the people of Lystra as well. Initially, they believed Paul and Barnabas to be gods and were willing to do *anything* for them. But later, they wanted to *kill* them. This is an experience that shows that those who were highly esteemed by men are often despised in the end. Before illness strikes, people cannot be humbled, and during sickness, they cannot be comforted. All of this proves the doctrine.

Now, regarding the reasons for this inordinacy, first, the primary cause is the Fall, which disrupted the natural order. As a result, the soul is like a musical instrument out of tune, where every note played is discordant, creating no harmony. Secondly, more immediate causes include a lack of sound judgment. People are unable to judge correctly, leading them to be bold when they should be cautious and fearful when they should be courageous. This happens because they lack the restraining influence of grace to keep their affections in check. Affections are like unruly horses that pull the soul off course unless guided by the hand of grace. When grace is absent, affections become even *more* disorderly, and this becomes an advantage for Satan. He takes advantage of our affections, adding fuel to the fire. Thus, his temptations arise when he sees our affections in turmoil.

The lesson here is to recognize the *inordinacy* of our affections. We have an inner inhabitant that is involved in every matter, and everything it does is amiss.

So, whatever you are engaged in, examine your affections. You will find that everything that originates from your flesh is awry. Be vigilant against sins, especially because they cloud judgment. When your affections are strong, be cautious.

You may wonder how to determine *if* your affections are inordinate. The answer lies in recognizing them as hindrances. All affections are planted by God for a specific purpose, utility, and benefit to humanity, not as hindrances. They serve a function and should not impede our actions. For instance, we cannot do without grief for past events or fear of future calamities, as they prompt us to take precautions. Similarly, anger motivates us to remove obstacles in our path. You can identify inordinate affections as you would diagnose a disease in medicine. Physicians follow a general rule: when there is *actio laesa*, meaning that the functions of nature are disrupted, they diagnose a disease. Likewise, in the soul, when grief hinders prayer and duty to God and others, it is inordinate. This was evident in the case of the Israelites, who couldn't heed Moses due to the grief in their hearts. As for anger, if it leads you to remove impediments in the way of virtuous desires, it is good. However, when it causes such disorder that you are inclined to argue with others and become less suitable for what is good, it is inordinate. The same applies to fear. If fear paralyzes your soul to the extent that you become incapable of preventing the feared evils and discourages you from God, it is inordinate. It makes you hide from God, just as Adam did, and as these people here wanted to do. If your joys and mirth make you less inclined and unprepared for prayer or good conversation, they are inordinate, acting as a damper on your happiness and hindering your spiritual progress.

You may ask, how can we resist the inordinacy of these affections? There are two ways: First, if your inordinate affection is due to a deficiency, such as not fearing when you should or not loving when you should, then you must strive to awaken it. We can sin as much by lacking affection as by misplacing it. Just as these people sinned both by not fearing before and by fearing the wrong things now, their fear was focused on the *judgment* rather than the *sin* itself. Had their fear been directed towards the sin, Samuel would not have needed to work hard to redirect them. Secondly, if you fear that God will no longer be reconciled to you, then your fear is misplaced, and that is sinful. Christ instructs us not to fear the things we will suffer but the sins that bring about these trials.

But what if your fears and affections have taken hold of your heart? How can you resist and rid your heart of them? First, rectify your judgments, as the distortion in your affections originates from your judgments. If you perceive certain things as evil and fear them excessively, seek enlightenment for your judgments. If you wonder how to do this, turn to the Word of God. The Word serves as a mirror, reflecting things as they truly are. I cannot provide specific verses for every affection, but consider *poverty*, which you fear. The Word diminishes its significance, as seen in Revelation 2:9, "I know thy poverty, but thou art rich." The Scriptures make only God's wrath and sin truly fearful. Therefore, cling to the Word and remind yourself that what you fear is merely your imagination. Regardless of whether your fears seem greater or lesser, the Word's verdict remains the same. Just as a garment may vary in size, the body underneath remains constant. Apply this principle to other aspects, such as the fear of losing reputation. We often fear these things, but the fault lies in our imagination. Align your heart with what the Word says.

Secondly, if these efforts do not succeed, turn to prayer. Inordinate affections create a significant disparity between a person when they are in and out of that state. It is akin to the difference between a drunken and a sober person. Prayer significantly composes the heart, bringing you into God's presence. Just as the sun disperses mist and fog, prayer dispels inordinate affections. Furthermore, seek communion with fellow believers. In such states, individuals are like feverish patients with distorted senses of taste. Allow the judgment and discernment of others to guide you.

Lastly, after all these steps, implore God to convince your judgment and fully persuade your understanding, as only He can do."

The second doctrine asserts that *the greatness of our sin does not hinder forgiveness.* Samuel explains that even though they have committed a great sin, he won't diminish it, but the Lord will still forgive them. This message is presented this way because people often struggle to believe this when they've sinned against their conscience *repeatedly*. They tend to be afraid to approach God, as we've seen through experience. Therefore, if anyone has committed a grave sin, they should take it to heart. It's true, they might have committed such a heinous act, but they should take comfort, humble themselves, and continue following the Lord. They will find that God will be as forgiving to them as He was to the people Samuel is addressing. The reasons for this are as follows:

First, the Gospel's pardon, which we preach, doesn't exclude any sin. Christ came *to save* sinners and to remove the sins of the world, and this is spoken without limitation. Second, the Gospel is preached to every creature without exception. There's no exclusion of any rebel or rebellion. Third, the price paid by Christ covers the greatest sins as well as the smallest ones. He is willing to forgive a thousand pounds upon satisfaction just as readily as ten groats. So, if you have Christ as your ransom, it doesn't matter how great or small your sins have been; the same price covers both. Fourth, the God we deal with is mighty, even in pardoning. In Micah 7:18, it says, "Who is like unto our God that pardoneth iniquity and passeth by the transgression of his heritage?" He will subdue them and *cast them into the depths of the sea*. This metaphor illustrates God's infinite capacity for forgiving transgressions. He demonstrates

His might in this act, and His mercy is divine, not human. Therefore, He uses the metaphor of casting sins into the depths of the sea because, just as the sea can engulf mountains as well as molehills, so can God's attributes and mercies. He delights in forgiving great sins because it distinguishes Him as God, not a mere human. He forgives more than a person is capable or willing to forgive.

Now, let's consider some examples. Adam's sin caused *the murder* of the entire world, making all men guilty of both the first and second death. Despite the severity of his sin and other aggravations like believing the devil over God, God provided a remedy and preached the Gospel to him in Gen. 3:15, which was not in vain. Similarly, Manasseh's sins exceeded all bounds, yet when he humbled himself profoundly, God showed him mercy and restored him to his kingdom. Even after reading about his sins, one might wonder why God would forgive him and reinstate him as if he had done nothing wrong. Not to mention the monstrous and heinous sins mentioned in 1 Corinthians 6:9, some of those guilty of such sins were washed and justified. "Such were some of you, but now are ye washed and justified."

The lesson here is that you should be careful not to limit the Holy One concerning His mercy. It's as great a sin to *restrict* God in His mercy as it is to limit Him in His power. Just as the Israelites limited God when they doubted His ability to bring them into Canaan due to the walls and giants, you should be cautious not to limit His mercy, thinking that your sins, no matter how heinous, are beyond forgiveness. If this is hard to accept, then go beyond your own judgment with faith, for our self-imposed limitations hinder us from believing. God's thoughts about pardoning are higher than ours, as stated in Isaiah 55.

Another point from these words is that the way to have a sin forgiven is to magnify it, not diminish it. Samuel, when comforting the people, not only magnified the sin but also God's mercies, thus comforting them. Therefore, the best way to have a sin forgiven is to confess it fully. First, it places you in a disposition where God has promised forgiveness because you realize your own vileness and inability to stand alone. You are emptied of self and understand that without God, you would perish. You are drawn away from yourself and everything in you, resting solely on God.

Secondly, confessing sin in detail brings more glory to God and shame to yourself. It also strengthens you against sin in the future. A full confession closes all avenues to the sin, whereas a partial confession allows room for continuing in sin.

The application is to teach you not to downplay your sins but to confess them fully. This might be a challenging duty, as people are reluctant to confess their sins when they are unwilling to let them go. Until one is determined to abandon a sin, they tend to downplay it. People also lack the light to see sin fully in its circumstances; we only see sin to the extent that the Holy Ghost enlightens us. As the light becomes brighter in a room, we can discern even the smallest specks.

Once again, thirdly, it's important to recognize that everyone has self-love within them. Therefore, when we perceive sin as our own, we are inclined to be lenient towards it. Just as Judah judged adultery worthy of death when he saw it in his daughter, but when it became his own sin, his stance changed. Similarly, David would have had a man put to death for stealing his neighbor's sheep, but when the same offense became his own, God had to humble him and make him confess. Therefore, when confessing your sins, it's essential to emphasize and acknowledge them fully. Say, "I have had access to these means, I have sinned against great light repeatedly, and I have broken the covenant I made with God." By doing this, you cannot go beyond the truth. As 1 John 3:20 states, "If our hearts condemn us, God is greater than our hearts."

Even if a person apprehends their sin fully, God conceives it even *more* comprehensively than we do. In this way, we should diligently search and take great care. Many sins that appear small at first may turn out to be significant, just like the sin of choosing a king that seemed harmless initially but, as Samuel tells them, led to *forsaking* the Lord, *abandoning* Samuel, and placing trust *in* kings. Similarly, David's numbering of the people seemed inconsequential, but he knew his own heart and realized his foolishness when he grasped his true intentions. Therefore, remember that the more you see sin abounding, the more you will see grace abounding. This will lead to increased love and appreciation for Christ, greater humility, and contentment in any circumstance.

Furthermore, it's important to note that one sin *paves the way* for another. Their sin nearly led them to completely depart from the Lord. This happens for several reasons:

First, every sinful act reinforces the habit of sin. Just as every act of grace strengthens the habit of grace, sin elevates the flesh above the spirit, ultimately gaining victory.

Second, every sin weakens the grace that should resist it. Like a disease not only has an opposing factor but also weakens the strength necessary for resistance, sin, especially great sins, seizes our strength and impairs our judgment, making it difficult to resist.

Third, committing a great sin discourages us from seeking pardon from God and *tempts* us to continue in sin. After committing a great sin, God may allow Satan to take "possession" of a person, as happened with Saul and Judas. Falling into sin makes it challenging to stop and leads to further sinning.

Therefore, we should treat sin as we would poison, not allowing it to remain in our system and taking an antidote as soon as possible.

Another point to observe is that discouragement and excessive fear are significant factors in our departure from God. Fear not and do not turn away from following the Lord. Many things deter us from coming to God, including strong lusts, procrastination in repentance, and, most importantly, excessive fear. Many people doubt that God will receive them due to their sinful nature and past failures, leading to discouragement.

Discouragement robs us of enthusiasm, effort, and even desire. If something seems hopeless, we are unlikely to pursue it. Likewise, when we view the Lord as a strict and severe Judge, we become distant from Him, content with the limited liberty we can enjoy without Him.

When we do approach the Lord, Satan bombards us with fears and objections. However, the Spirit encourages us, saying, "Do not fear." We must choose whether to align with Satan or the Spirit. Christ invites us to come to Him for rest, reassuring us that our sins are not insurmountable burdens. Yet, Satan's goal in presenting these objections is to discourage us.

If you wonder whether these objections are from Satan or based on a right assessment of your condition, remember that if they push you further away from the Lord and make you *apathetic* towards prayer and repentance, they are from Satan.

In the face of committing great sins, it is your duty and the wisest course of action to turn to God immediately. When Samuel assured the people not to fear, they might have asked, "What should we do?" His response was clear: "Turn not aside from following the Lord your God, but serve Him with all your hearts." Therefore, it is imperative that when you commit significant sins, you *promptly* turn back to God.

The Spirit, through Samuel's command, makes it their duty, and it is the wisest course to follow divine commands. The reasons for this are as follows:

Firstly, the heart immediately begins to harden after committing a sin, and the longer it remains unrepentant, the harder it becomes. However, if you address it promptly, the wound can be healed sooner, and the pain will be lessened.

Secondly, committing one sin exposes you to more significant sins. It's like breaking down the walls; the longer the breach remains open, the more enemies can enter. A gap is created that, if left unchecked, allows good things to escape and evil to enter. David is an example; had he humbled himself and renewed his repentance, he could have prevented the subsequent murder of Uriah and other sins.

Thirdly, the longer you persist in an unrepented sin, the greater the sin becomes because you abuse God's patience. He considers every hour, and His delay is not due to slackness but patience. Abusing His patience adds to His wrath with each passing moment.

Fourthly, the same duties you were bound to perform before are still incumbent upon you. Your sin is not an excuse to omit them. Therefore, turning from your sin is the best course of action.

Objection: Some may ask if a person must immediately enter God's presence after grossly offending Him.

Answer: Yes, you may and should do so, but not with the same disposition that led you to commit the sin. Instead, come with a humbled heart, turned toward God, deeply aware of your sin, and committed to new obedience. Coming in promptly under these conditions is not unreasonable. Imagine a rebel who, after rebelling, enters a king's presence with a sword in hand; he should not expect pardon. But if he comes meekly with a rope around his neck, he may find mercy. Moreover, it's worth noting that the heart is more easily turned if you take advantage of it immediately after committing the sin. There are two objections to consider:

First objection: You may say that your heart cannot be humbled enough immediately.

Response: God does not demand a specific level of humiliation to accept you. If you recognize and acknowledge your sin, view yourself as vile, and resolve not to return to it, even in a small measure, the Lord accepts you in Christ.

Secondly, you may think that you cannot be as humbled as you'd like at first. In that case, add to your humility afterward, as David did when he said, "Lord, I have sinned." God forgave him, even though he was not as deeply humbled as he would later become.

Objection 2: Some may argue that their sin may not be healed yet, so they cannot come with confidence, and their hearts may remain as false as ever.

Answer: It's important to understand that you should seek pardon first, and then prepare for healing. A reliable rule is that there is no healing of sin until there is assurance of forgiveness. The Lord not only washes away guilt but also heals the stain and gives a new Spirit. This is part of His covenant (Jeremiah 31, Ezekiel 36). Merely making a resolution against sin is not enough; you must take *action* to heal it. When you have fallen into sin, don't think you can improve the situation by continuing on the wrong path or standing still. Instead, return and serve the Lord, for He remains the same God, and His bond still obligates you to serve Him. You might wonder where else you could go, but there is no hope in creatures; they are vain and won't deliver you. Return to the Lord, for He will not forsake His people, and He won't forsake His name.

Furthermore, observe that the sins we commit do not change the Lord in any substantial way. They may make Him angry, and you may feel the effects of it, *but He remains the same God*. Our sins do not break the covenant or void it. God is the same, and you are covenantally the same; your hearts are the same justified hearts toward Him, and His love for you remains. Sins do not bring about new and substantial alteration in God or in His relationship with you. He is faithful, when we are faithless and fall and stumble.

The lesson is that you should not believe that the Lord will reject you when you have sinned. Our Savior, Jesus Christ, conveyed the same message through the parable of the Prodigal Son, illustrating God's willingness to receive sinners. When David said, "I have sinned," God responded, "I have put away your sin." Likewise, after Peter's denial, Christ looked upon him with the same familiarity as before. However, do not think that God will hold the wicked innocent; if you have *deceitful hearts*, forgiveness will not be granted.

Consider how deserving of utter destruction those are who refuse to turn to the Lord, even when He is so ready to receive those who have offended Him. If God were to say to someone, "You have committed this sin against me, but come in, and there shall be no hindrance on my part, unless the stubbornness of your own will hinders you," who would not say that the one who refuses is worthy of condemnation? Christ is said to come to render vengeance to those who do not obey the Gospel, and therefore, Samuel adds that if they forsake the Lord, they and their king shall perish.

# The New Life

"He that hath the Son hath life; and he that hath not the Son of God hath not life." (1Jo. 5:12).

The Apostle's purpose here is to explain the great privileges we receive through Jesus Christ, one of which is that having the Son means *having* the gift of grace in the present and eternal life in glory. This is contrasted with the opposite: not having the Son means lacking this life. Therefore, it's clear that if someone lacks spiritual life in the present, *they are not in Christ*, but if they possess it, *they are in Christ and will live eternally*. Two important points should be noted:

First, every person is naturally spiritually dead, specifically in terms of sin and wrongdoing.

Second, there is an opportunity for a different life that opposes this death.

Let's address the first point. Every person is born spiritually dead, not being part of the last Adam, but rather as a member of the old Adam. In this sense, they are born spiritually dead, even though they have natural life. If the root (representing the old Adam) is dead, then all the branches that stem from it are also dead. Spiritual life is essentially a connection between the soul and the Spirit of God, much like natural life is a connection between the body and the soul. When the soul departs from the body, just as the Holy Spirit withdraws from the soul when it becomes disjointed, disturbed, and unfit for use.

This is similar to how a person dwells in a house while it is habitable, plays a musical instrument while it is in proper condition, and uses a vessel when it is intact. However, when the house becomes dilapidated, the inhabitant departs; when the instrument is out of tune, it is set aside, and when the vessel is broken, it is discarded. Likewise, the soul departs from the body when it deteriorates due to a mortal disease, and similarly, the Holy Spirit withdraws from the soul of a person when it is corrupted and troubled by the mortal disease of sin and natural corruption. This is the state of *every* natural person until they are renewed through the infusion of a new life by being born again.

It's a common belief among natural individuals that if they attend church, get baptized, pray, listen to the word of God, embrace true religion, and perform its outward duties, they are *undoubtedly* in a state of spiritual life. However, it's crucial to make it clear that unless people become *new creatures and are born again*, they remain in a state of spiritual death and cannot be saved in that condition. Those without spiritual life also lack the Son, and they face eternal damnation, as Christ stated in John 3.

Ephesians 4:18 mentions that people are estranged from this life due to their ignorance and hardened hearts, "Having the understanding darkened, being alienated from the life of God through the ignorance that is in them, because of the blindness of their heart." This estrangement is due to ignorance because they are unaware of the work of life and regeneration. They believe there is more latitude in religion than there actually is and assume they can be saved by being less strict and zealous, *not* realizing what true spiritual life entails. Their ignorance leads them to be strangers to this life. Additionally, the hardness of their hearts contributes to this estrangement. Their hearts are either preoccupied with worldly matters, preventing them from focusing on spiritual life, or saturated with worldly pleasures and delights, making them oblivious to spiritual matters. Consequently, they are strangers to this life, unable to judge whether they possess the grace of spiritual life.

To determine whether they are spiritually dead or alive, individuals can examine the characteristics of life and death, similar to those found in the analogy of natural life and death. A significant change should be evident in those who have been transformed from spiritual death to life. While various changes occur in a person's life, such as aging, experiencing different environments and company, and adapting to education and customs, the transformation from spiritual death to life is profound. It can be described as a change so significant that it feels as if a different soul resides in the same body. This transformed individual can confidently declare, "I am not who I used to be," when confronted with old temptations, lusts, and acquaintances. Even though these old influences may persist, the transformed person is not the same and is not found by those who seek the old version.

Just as grafting onto a crab apple tree changes the sap, fruit, leaves, and overall appearance of the tree, the infusion of the life of grace into a natural person brings about a profound change in both their inner and outer selves. This change affects the entire framework of the soul. However, it's important to understand that this change is not superficial; it involves the obliteration of the old sinful nature and the infusion of supernatural qualities of grace and holiness. This infusion is essential for genuine righteousness to flourish. Just as the earth can naturally produce grass and wildflowers but must be plowed and sown to yield choice plants, common human natures can exhibit morally good behavior but require plowing and sowing for true righteousness to emerge. Plowing involves breaking the heart with an awareness of sin and God's eternal wrath. The heart must be seen as spiritually dead, and individuals should be pierced and wounded by this realization, similar to those in Acts 2 who were *pricked in their hearts* and sought salvation. Sowing involves the implantation of spiritual graces that transform and renew individuals, as described in Romans 12:2, where they are called to be changed through the renewal of their minds. This is one way to determine whether one is spiritually dead or alive.

Secondly, when there is no action, when there is no motion in a person, we say they are *dead*. When a person does nothing savingly, when they do not stir themselves, we consider them as *spiritually dead*. Now, this is the condition of every natural person; they are unable to move a hand or foot in the ways of true godliness.

If you argue that they are able to do something, they can pray, hear the Word, receive the Sacrament, and perform excellent acts of justice and righteousness among people, I respond, that is indeed true, but the Scripture speaks of certain "dead works," as mentioned in Hebrews 9:14, where "The blood of Christ" is said to "purge our consciences from dead works." These works can be done by natural individuals, and they are good in themselves, having the appearance of genuinely good deeds (similar to how a lifeless body may resemble a living one). However, they are truly "dead works," meaning they may seem golden on the outside and appear beautiful to the doer and others, but in reality, they are "abominable in the sight of God." Therefore, a natural person *may* fulfill certain duties and obey God to a certain extent, but they do so with counterfeit currency that looks genuine but is made of base metal. I recall a story told by Remigius, a judge in Loraine, who condemned many witches on their own confessions. He mentioned that the devil had given them boxes filled with what appeared to be current coins, but when they tried to use them, they discovered they were nothing but withered leaves. Similarly, Satan deceives natural individuals in matters of greater importance, allowing them to think well of the good works and duties they perform, making them believe they are genuine. However, when they try to use this treasure on the day of death or during times of extremity and judgment, they find that these works are nothing more than withered leaves, unacceptable to God.

The Apostle speaks in 1 Timothy 3 of certain individuals who had "a form of godliness" but denied its power. These people performed formal and customary acts of goodness and dutiful actions that satisfied their consciences due to their ignorance and inability to judge. Satan deals with people in this manner, as adults do with children. We take real gold and silver from them and appease them with counters. In the same way, Satan endeavors to prevent people from performing good works and holy duties wholeheartedly. Instead, he satisfies their consciences with a *form of godliness* that lacks *its true power.*

You may wonder how to discern whether good works, which are inherently good, are genuinely good when performed by an individual. I offer two criteria:

First, it is certain that unless these actions are vital, meaning they originate from an inner principle of life, they are not good deeds in the eyes of the Lord. Just as there are movements in clocks and watches that do not stem from life but from artifice, the same applies to matters of religion. Many good actions may be carried out, and many virtuous inclinations towards godliness may arise, yet they may not originate from the life of grace but from external considerations such as fear of hell, fear of judgment, the prospect of death, or calamity during sickness. In such cases, people may be prompted to perform these actions, but just as the wheels of a clock cease their motion when the spring is unwound, these good fits of godliness often end when the initial impetus is removed. Therefore, to determine whether your works are genuine and acceptable to God on the last day, consider whether they arise from an *internal principle*, a principle of life within.

Secondly, you can recognize them by their lack of warmth, for *coldness* is a sign of death. When these good works are performed by a natural person, there is no life, no warmth, no vitality, and no enthusiasm in them. In contrast, fervent prayer is said to be powerful (James 5), and Romans 12 exhorts us to be "fervent in spirit, serving the Lord." Good deeds lacking warmth and fire are not acknowledged by God. This is because if there is no heat, *there is no presence of His Spirit*. Our prayers, in such cases, are merely the words of our own spirits, and the works we do are dead works because they are the products and effects of dead flesh without the Holy Spirit. Jesus spoke of baptizing with the Holy Ghost and with fire, indicating that the Holy Spirit is like fire. Therefore, holy individuals are often described as fire, as Chrysostom said, Peter appeared as if made of fire walking among stubble. When asked about Basil, it was said he was presented in a dream as a pillar of fire with the motto, "Such a one was Basil." Similarly, when Latimer was questioned about the prevalence of preaching compared to practicing, he responded, "Deest ignis," *fire is lacking*. The same can be said in this case; many good duties, such as prayer, hearing, receiving the Sacrament, and worshiping God, may be performed. However, consider whether they lack the liveliness and fervor that the Spirit of God requires. Reflect on whether they are performed without warmth or are only partially carried out, much like Hosea's cake ("Ephraim is a cake not turned," (Hosea 7:8), and if so, they are *dead* works. In contrast, true private prayer between God and us warms and enlivens the heart, aligns it with grace, and sets it right before God. Genuine hearing ignites a fire within us that burns away sinful lusts and corrupt affections. Therefore, the second means by which we can determine whether we are alive in righteousness or dead in sin is to consider whether we experience any motions and, if so, what kind of actions they are.

Furthermore, you can discern it by considering what you contend for most. Life is precious, and every creature strives to preserve it, willing to part with anything rather than lose it. Similarly, a person who possesses the life of grace values it above all else. They will endure anything, even the loss of life, possessions, liberty, or anything else, rather than wound their conscience, violate their inner peace, or disrupt their communion with God. These aspects are as dear and sweet to them as life itself. On the other hand, another person contends fiercely for their lusts, profit, reputation, pleasures, and even their sins. They would rather endure the loss of a clear conscience and engage in irregular behavior towards God and others than be hindered in these pursuits because these pursuits constitute their life. They are dead to Christ and alive to sin.

Similarly, the quality of life is determined by the nature of one's desires and actions. If a person lives a life of sin, which the Scriptures refer to as spiritual death, their inner thoughts and affections revolve around carnal pleasures. They either find solace in reminiscing about past pleasures, indulge in present ones, or anticipate future carnal delights. On the other hand, someone who lives a life of grace finds the opposite to be more appealing. Every form of life naturally attracts what is most suitable and agreeable to it, like food that sustains it and brings delight. *Pleasure*, "voluptas," can be described as the application of what is suitable and agreeable to us.

Now, you might argue that natural individuals can engage in activities like hearing, reading, and praying, which are considered holy exercises.

I agree; indeed, these activities are virtuous and commendable and should not be neglected. However, they are not sufficient on their own unless they nurture us and help us grow. As it is written in 1 Peter 2, "Desire the sincere milk of the word, that you may grow thereby." It is not enough to merely *show* the meat; we must also *see the man*. Christ, the great Shepherd of the sheep, is interested in the same way shepherds are, not in the hay given to the sheep but in the wool and the milk. In other words, He is interested in the *fruits* and *effects* of all our hearing and praying. A person may engage in these duties, but without spiritual life and an internal transformative process, these actions may not nourish them, cause growth, or provide strength. Instead, they might be like a person suffering from atrophy, who eats a lot but remains as lean and weak as if they hadn't eaten at all. The Scriptures refer to such individuals as having "a name to live but are dead," and they are "always learning but never come to the knowledge of the truth," meaning they *lack* true spiritual life.

Now, regarding the final characteristic of life, just as every form of life attracts what is suitable and pleasing to it, it also expels and opposes whatever is contrary and harmful. Likewise, a person who possesses spiritual life in Christ, even though they may still have remnants and traces of sin within them, despises and fights against those sinful elements continuously. They resist sin as health opposes sickness or as a living fountain rejects the mud that falls into it. They work tirelessly to expel it and do not rest until they are purified. In contrast, others reject the good thoughts and motions that are kindled within them (for they may experience moments of goodness and righteousness).

They become weary of these inclinations and of the means that would increase them, and they do not find contentment until they immerse themselves in sinful pursuits that align with their disposition, upbringing, or customs. These sins they allow to persist without opposition or resistance, much like mud in stagnant ponds. It's essential to note that this is a significant sign of spiritual death. I would dare say that if we persist in any known sin, that is, if we continually engage in a particular sinful behavior that we acknowledge as wrong, *it is dangerous and potentially fatal*, as one dominant disease can be just as lethal as many. If a swine wallows in one dirty puddle, it becomes unclean all over, as if it had wallowed in more. Scripture is explicit on this matter, as seen in 2 Corinthians 5:17, "Whosoever is in Christ is a new creature: old things are passed away; behold, all things are become new." Furthermore, Galatians 5:24 declares, "And they that are Christ's have crucified the flesh with the affections and lusts." Therefore, if even one sinful desire *remains alive* in a person, it is evidence that the entire body of sin is still active within them. In such a case, they remain in a state of spiritual death and have not yet experienced the "glorious liberty of the Sons of God." In this way, I have demonstrated that every individual, by nature, is spiritually dead in sins and trespasses, how to recognize it, and that unless we undergo the first resurrection, we will not partake in the second.

Now, let us turn to the second aspect: there is a form of life that opposes this death. To understand it, one must recognize that every person, by nature, is in a state of spiritual slumber. Consequently, they cannot perceive, feel, or acknowledge this spiritual death. Just as a dead person cannot sense their own death, those lacking spiritual life are not conscious of it. This contrast is essential because the first step to rescue a person from this dreadful state of death is to awaken them, open their eyes to see that they are children of wrath, and make them aware of their desperate need for Jesus Christ. They should seek and long for Him as a condemned person yearns for a pardon or as someone pursued by an avenger of blood seeks refuge in a city of safety. This awakening is crucial, as emphasized in Ephesians 5:14, "Awake thou that sleepest, and arise from the dead." Therefore, the initial work of God in saving a person is to rouse them from spiritual slumber, lay the burden of sin on their conscience, and set it on them like the avenger of blood chasing them. Once this awakening takes place, the individual will flee to the city of refuge, namely, to Christ, as Joab sought refuge at the horns of the altar, earnestly crying out for the pardon of their sins. This cry is as desperate as Samson's plea for water In Judges 15, "now shall I die for thirst," (Judges 15:18). When a person comes to Christ in this humbled state, Christ accepts them and breathes the breath of life into them, just as God breathed life into Adam. This infusion of new life and power from Christ is what transforms them into a living person. As stated in John 5:29, "The time shall come, when the dead shall hear the voice of the Son of God, and they that hear it shall live." In *this* context, spiritually dead individuals *will hear* the voice of the Son of God, and those who heed His call will receive life. When a person touches Christ by faith, similar to how the woman touched the hem of His garment, a virtue flows from Him that heals the soul, much like the virtue that healed her of her blood issue. It's worth noting that just as iron is drawn to a lodestone when brought near, despite the physical distance between Christ in heaven and us on earth, a certain virtue emanates from Him, drawing us toward Him and changing and revitalizing us through the transmission of His divine power.

Now, let's turn to the second aspect: that there exists a life that is in direct opposition to this death. To understand this life, consider that every person, by nature, *is in a deep spiritual slumber*. Consequently, they do not see, feel, or acknowledge this spiritual death. Just as a dead person is unaware of their condition, one lacking this spiritual life is not conscious of it. However, this is not the case with the body.

You might wonder, 'What kind of power is this? What sort of infusion and transmission is it?' My beloved, it's true that this is the profound mystery of spiritual life and regeneration. However, we will endeavor to explain it to the extent possible. It operates in the following manner: just as an artisan, while crafting a work of art, exerts an influence from the skill residing in their mind that shapes and molds the work, impressing upon it the idea conceived within; or, as we observe the will directing the body's movements, with a commanding and active power emanating from the will to govern the members according to the will's disposition; or, as we see in the works of nature, with bees constructing their combs and birds building their nests under the instinctual guidance of God, the author of nature. Such is the virtue and power the Scriptures refer to as the virtue of Christ's resurrection, coming from Christ and the Spirit of Christ. It molds and shapes the heart, exercises commanding power within, guides and directs, enabling the individual to act in accordance with God's will. This is what the Apostle alludes to in Ephesians 1:19 when he prays that their "eyes might be opened, that they might see the exceeding greatness of his power that works in those that believe." Notice that it is described as *power*— not an empty form of godliness but an effective and prevailing power. It not only adorns us with the outward appearance of a good profession but *dyes the heart* in the colors of grace *and* holiness. It not only alters the surface but transforms the entire heart, reorients the course of life, and directs it toward a completely different destination on the moral compass. This power differs from the mere form of godliness previously mentioned in the sense that life differs from a picture, substance from shadow, and that which has sinews and efficacy from that which is weak and powerless. The power and virtue that emanates from Christ and the Spirit of Christ when God intends to grant someone spiritual life doesn't merely offer empty promises, instilling desires and purposes that lack the strength to come to fruition. Instead, it implants them in the heart so that they thrive there, just as creatures thrive in their natural habitats. In contrast, in those who retain their old hearts and natures, such desires wither and vanish, much like plants in unsuitable soil. Therefore, to determine whether this life has been wrought in us, we must consider whether we have ever experienced such a powerful and virtuous influence from Christ that *changes, renews, and empowers us*, enabling not only the *willingness* to live a holy life, mortify our lusts, pray fervently, and keep the Sabbath with delight but also the ability to *carry* out these actions. This is akin to what the Apostle declares, "I can do all things through Christ which strengtheneth me," (Philippians 4:13).

Now, let us be encouraged to believe in the existence of such a life. For it is written, 'This life is hidden with Christ in God' (Colossians 3). It is hidden, and therefore it must be believed because we do not need to believe things we can see. To understand why it is described as hidden, consider two aspects:

1. From whom it is hidden.
2. With what it is hidden.

Let's start with the first aspect: from whom is this life hidden?"

It is hidden from *natural* men, just as colors are hidden from a blind man or as they are hidden in the dark. The colors exist, but they are hidden from man because either he lacks the ability to see them, like a blind person, or he lacks the necessary light to perceive them, like in darkness.

Furthermore, what is it hidden with? This spiritual life, this life of grace, is concealed within our natural life. We see people breathe and live, but this spiritual life is within them, invisible to our eyes.

Additionally, it is concealed beneath an unimpressive exterior, just as Christ was hidden under the humble guise of a carpenter's son. Similarly, the wisdom of God is hidden beneath the apparent foolishness of preaching. Those whom the world did not consider worthy were hidden under the coverings of sheep-skins and goat-skins, as mentioned in Hebrews 11. The weighty mysteries of salvation are hidden beneath the simple elements of bread and wine in the sacrament. In a similar manner, this life is hidden, often under an unimpressive exterior because many who live this life of grace appear base and unimportant in the world's eyes. This is another factor that conceals this life from us.

Thirdly, it is concealed by the weaknesses of the saints, just as you can see this natural life hidden during unconsciousness or as reason is obscured during drunkenness. There is life and reason present, but they are not evident. It cannot be denied that even the holiest individuals have many imperfections, as seen in the experiences of figures like David and Peter. Because of these imperfections, we may fail to recognize this spiritual life, sometimes *even* believing there is no life in those who possess it.

Lastly, this life is obscured by false reports, just as Christ was hidden from the world when He was falsely reported as a wine-bibber and a companion of gluttons, or as one who cast out demons through Beelzebub, the Prince of Devils. The same kind of concealment occurred with the Apostle Paul and other apostles when they were reported as deceivers despite being true men. Therefore, those in prominent positions should be cautious about giving credence to false reports. Throughout history, people, especially good individuals, have often been misreported, while evil people receive better reports. Relying on these reports can lead us to justify the wicked and condemn the righteous. Therefore, in all these ways, this life remains hidden from us, and that's why we must believe in it, even though we may find some support through personal experiences.

We can observe that there is a group of people whose lives do not revolve around carnal pleasures and sinful indulgences, which means there *must be* another life they live, an inward and hidden life, which is concealed with Christ in God.

Moreover, we can see another group of people who are willing to endure torture, imprisonment, and even death. They wouldn't willingly relinquish their natural lives if they didn't have hope in a better life, a life they value more. Our own experiences can help confirm our faith in this spiritual life.

This leads us to the first practical application: we *must believe* in the existence of this life.

Secondly, if not having this life means one is not in Christ, then it's crucial for us to exhibit the *fruits and effects* of this spiritual life in our actions. We should experience the transformation we've discussed earlier, showing a strong inclination to live according to God's will, an ability to forsake known sins, and a genuine love for our fellow believers. The latter, love for the brethren, is emphasized in the Bible as a primary sign of this spiritual life, as mentioned in 1 John 3:14.

Let us understand that living this life is of utmost importance, and those who have greater power and opportunities to do good should take special heed. The welfare of the Church should be our concern. As one Church is as precious as another, and if we love any Church, we should love them all.

We should also consider that our help for other churches is an investment in our own safety, following the principle that what we give to others, especially in their times of distress, often returns to us in our moments of need. Neglecting this duty can have consequences, but assisting the Church will surely bring blessings.

Lastly, we are encouraged to *live* this life of grace, which involves *performing acts of obedience to God's commandments*. This spiritual life is sustained and nourished through obedience to God's commands. Just as we need food to sustain our physical lives, the life of grace thrives when we follow God's instructions.

In conclusion, we are urged to believe in this hidden spiritual life, to exhibit its fruits through love and good deeds, to care for the welfare of the Church, and to continue living the life of grace by following God's commandments. May God work this life of grace in those who lack it and strengthen it in those who possess it.

# Other Works Published by Puritan Publications

1647 Westminster Confession of Faith 3rd Edition – KJV Bible
A Biblical Response to Superstition, Will-Worship and the Christmas Holiday – by Daniel Cawdrey (1588-1664)
A Devotional on Our Savior's Death and Passion by Charles Herle (1598-1659)
A Discourse on Church Discipline and Reformation – by Daniel Cawdrey (1588-1664)
A Glimpse of God's Glory – Thomas Hodges (1600-1672)
A Golden Topaz, or Heart-Jewel, Namely, a Conscience Purified and Pacified by the Blood and Spirit of Christ – by Francis Whiddon (d. 1656) 2nd Ed.
A Sermon Against Lukewarmness in Religion – by Henry Wilkinson (1566-1647)
A Treatise of the Loves of Christ to His Spouse by Samuel Bolton, D.D. (1606-1654)
A Treatise on Divine Contentment – by Simeon Ashe (d. 1662)
A Vindication of the Keys of the Kingdom of Heaven into the Hands of the Right Owners – by Daniel Cawdrey (1588-1664)
Armilla Catechetica, or a Chain of Theological Principles – by John Arrowsmith (1602-1659)
Attending the Lord's Table – by Henry Tozer (1602-1650)
Christ Inviting Sinners to Come to Him for Rest – by Jeremiah Burroughs (1599-1646)
Christ the Settlement in Unsettled Times – Jeremiah Whitaker (1599–1654)
Ezra's Covenant Renewal and the Pursuit of a Lasting Reformation - by Josiah Shute (1588-1643)
Family Reformation Promoted, and Other Works – by Daniel Cawdrey (1588-1664)
God is Our Refuge and Our Strength by George Gipps (n.d.)
God Paying Every Man His Due – Francis Woodcock (1614-1649)
God With Us, and Other Works – by John Strickland (1601-1670)
God, the Best Acquaintance of Christians – by Matthew Newcomen (1610–1669)
God's Voice from His Throne of Glory – by John Carter (d. 1655)

Gospel Peace, Or Four Useful Discourses – by Jeremiah Burroughs (1599-1646)
Gospel Worship, or, The Right Manner of Sanctifying the name of God in General, in Hearing the Word, Receiving the Lord's Supper, and Prayer by Jeremiah Burroughs (1599-1646)
Gradual Reformation Intolerable – by C. Matthew McMahon and Anthony Burgess (1600-1663)
Halting Stigmatized – by Arthur Sallaway (b. 1606)
How to Serve God in Private and Public Worship – by John Jackson (1600-1648)
Independency A Great Schism – by Daniel Cawdrey (1588-1664)
Jacob's Seed and David's Delight – by Jeremiah Burroughs (1599-1646)
Jesus Christ God's Shepherd – by William Strong (d. 1654)
Making Religion One's Business – by Herbert Palmer (1601-1647)
Presumptive Regeneration, or, the Baptismal Regeneration of Elect Infants – by Cornelius Burgess (1589-1665)
Primitive Baptism and Therein Infant's and Parent's Rights by Matthew Sylvester (1636–1708)
Real Thankfulness – by Simeon Ashe (d. 1662)
Reasonable Christianity – by Henry Hammond (1605-1660)
Reformation and Desolation – by Stephen Marshall (1594–1655)
Regeneration and the New Birth – by Isaac Ambrose (1604–1663)
Repentance and Fasting – by Peter Du Moulin (1601-1684) and Henry Wilkinson (1566-1647)
Rules for Our Walking With God – by Jeremiah Burroughs (1599-1646)
Salvation in a Mystery – by John Bond (1612-1676)
Scripture's Self Evidence – by Thomas Ford (1598-1674)
Selected Works of Peter Sterry – by Peter Sterry (1613-1672)
Sermons, Prayers, and Pulpit Addresses – Alexander Henderson (1583-1646)
Singing of Psalms the Duty of Christians – by Thomas Ford (1598–1674)
Spots of the Godly and of the Wicked – by Jeremiah Burroughs (1599-1646)
The All-Seeing Unseen Eye of God and Other Sermons – by Matthew Newcomen (1610–1669)
The Art of Divine Meditation by Edmund Calamy (1600-1666)
The Art of Happiness – by Francis Rous (1579-1659)

The Certainty of Heavenly and the Uncertainty of Earthly Treasures – by William Strong (d. 1654)
The Christian's Duty Towards Reformation – by Thomas Ford (1598–1674)
The Church's Need of Jesus Christ – by Thomas Valentine (1586-1665)
The Comfort of Christ to Weak Believers – by John Durant (1620-1686)
The Covenant of Life Opened – by Samuel Rutherford (1600-1661)
The Covenant of Works and the Covenant of Grace – by Edmund Calamy (1600-1666)
The Covenant-Avenging Sword Brandished – by John Arrowsmith (1602-1659)
The Difficulties of and Encouragements to a Reformation – Anthony Burgess (1600-1663) 2nd Ed.
The Doctrine of Man's Future Eternity – by John Jackson (1600-1648)
The Efficiency of God's Grace in Bringing Gain-Saying Sinners to Christ – by Simeon Ashe (d. 1662)
The Eternity and Certainty of Hell's Torments – by William Strong (d. 1654)
The Excellency of Holy Courage in Evil Times – by Jeremiah Burroughs (1599-1646)
The Excellent Name of God – by Jeremiah Burroughs (1599-1646)
The Fall of Adam and Other Works – by John Greene (d. 1660)
The Glorious Name of God the Lord of Hosts by Jeremiah Burroughs (1599-1646)
The Glory and Beauty of God's Portion and Other Sermons – by Gaspar Hickes, (d. 1677)
The Godly Man's Ark – by Edmund Calamy (1600-1666)
The Growth and Spreading of Heresy – by Thomas Hodges (1600-1672)
The Guard of the Tree of Life, a Discourse on the Sacraments – by Samuel Bolton (1606-1654)
The Light of Faith and Way of Holiness – by Richard Byfield (1598–1664)
The Manifold Wisdom of God Seen in Covenant Theology – by George Walker (1581-1651)
The Nature, Danger and Cure of Temptation by Richard Capel (1586–1656)

The Necessity, Dignity and Duty of Gospel Ministers – by Thomas Hodges (1600-1672)

The Rock of Israel and Other Sermons – by Edmund Staunton (1600-1671)

The Saint's Communion with God – by William Strong, A.M. (d. 1654)

The Saint's Inheritance and the Worldling's Portion – by Jeremiah Burroughs (1599-1646)

The Saint's Will Judge the World, and Other Sermons – by Daniel Cawdrey (1588-1664)

The Sermons of William Spurstowe (1605-1666)

The Soul's Porter, or a Treatise on the Fear of God – by William Price (1597-1646)

The Spiritual Chemyst, or Divine Meditations on Several Subjects – by William Spurstowe (1605-1666)

The Sweetness of Divine Meditation by William Bridge (1600-1670)

The Trial of a Christian's Sincere Love to Christ – by William Pinke (1599–1629)

The Wells of Salvation Opened – by William Spurstowe (1605-1666)

The Works of Richard Greenham Volume 1 – by Richard Greenham (1531-1594)

The Worthy Churchman, or the Faithful Minister of Jesus Christ – by John Jackson (1600-1648)

The Zealous Christian – by Simeon Ashe (d. 1662)

Truth, the Great Business of Our Times – by John Maynard (1600-1665)

Zeal for God's House Quickened – by Oliver Bowles B.D. (1574-1664?)

Zion's Joy – Jeremiah Burroughs (1599-1646)